1 3 5 7 9 10 8 6 4 2

Vintage
20 Vauxhall Bridge Road,
London SW1V 2SA

Vintage Classics is part of the Penguin Random House
group of companies whose addresses can be found at
global.penguinrandomhouse.com

Penguin
Random House
UK

*The Standard Edition of the Complete Psychological Works of Sigmund Freud,
Volume IV: The Interpretation of Dreams (First Part)* first published in Great
Briatin by The Hogarth Press in 1953; reprinted with corrections in 1958
The Essentials of Psycho-Analysis first published in Great Britain by The
Hogarth Press in 1986
This short edition published by Vintage in 2018

penguin.co.uk/vintage

ISBN 9781784874094

Typeset in 9.5/14.5 pt FreightText Pro
by Jouve (UK), Milton Keynes
Printed and bound by Clays Ltd, St Ives plc

Dreams

SIGMUND FREUD

VINTAGE MINIS

On Dreams

(1901)[1]

I

DURING THE EPOCH which may be described as pre-scientific, men had no difficulty in finding an explanation of dreams. When they remembered a dream after waking up, they regarded it as either a favourable or a hostile manifestation by higher powers, daemonic and divine. When modes of thought belonging to natural science began to flourish, all this ingenious mythology was transformed into psychology, and to-day only a small minority of educated people doubt that dreams are a product of the dreamer's own mind.

Since the rejection of the mythological hypothesis, however, dreams have stood in need of explanation. The conditions of their origin, their relation to waking mental life, their dependence upon stimuli which force their way upon perception during the state of sleep, the many peculiarities of their content which are repugnant to waking thought, the inconsistency between their ideational images and the affects attaching to them, and lastly their transitory character, the manner in which waking thought pushes them on one side as something alien to it, and mutilates or extinguishes them in memory – all of these and other problems besides have been awaiting clarification for many hundreds of years, and till now no satisfactory solution of them has been advanced. But what stands in the foreground of our interest is the question of the *significance* of dreams, a question which bears a double sense. It inquires in the first place as to the psychical significance of dreaming, as to the relation of dreams to other mental processes, and as to any biological function that they may have; in the second place it seeks to discover whether dreams can be interpreted, whether the content of individual dreams has a 'meaning', such as we are accustomed to find in other psychical structures.

In the assessment of the significance of dreams three lines of thought can be distinguished. One of these, which echoes, as it were, the ancient overvaluation of dreams, is expressed in the writings of certain philosophers. They consider that the basis of dream-life is a peculiar state of mental activity, and even go so far as to acclaim that state as an elevation to a higher level. For instance, Schubert [1814] declares that dreams are a liberation of the spirit from the power of external nature, and a freeing of the soul from the bonds of the senses. Other thinkers, without going so far as this, insist nevertheless that dreams arise essentially from mental impulses and represent manifestations of mental forces which have been prevented from expanding freely during the day-time. (Cf. the 'dream imagination' of Scherner [1861, 97 f.] and Volkelt [1875, 28 f.].) A large number of observers agree in attributing to dream-life a capacity for superior functioning in certain departments at least (e.g. in memory).

In sharp contrast to this, the majority of medical writers adopt a view according to which dreams scarcely reach the level of being psychical phenomena at all. On their theory, the sole instigators of dreams are the sensory and somatic stimuli which either impinge upon the sleeper from outside or become active accidentally in his internal organs. What is dreamt, they contend, has no more claim to sense and meaning than, for instance, the sounds which would be produced if 'the ten fingers of a man who knows nothing of music were wandering over the keys of a piano'. [Strümpell, 1877, 84.] Dreams are described by Binz [1878, 35] as being no more than 'somatic processes which are in every case useless and in many cases positively pathological'. All the characteristics of dream-life would thus be explained as being due to the disconnected activity of separate organs or groups of cells in an otherwise sleeping brain, an activity forced upon them by physiological stimuli.

Popular opinion is but little affected by this scientific

judgement, and is not concerned as to the sources of dreams; it seems to persist in the belief that nevertheless dreams have a meaning, which relates to the prediction of the future and which can be discovered by some process of interpretation of a content which is often confused and puzzling. The methods of interpretation employed consist in transforming the content of the dream as it is remembered, either by replacing it piecemeal in accordance with a fixed key, or by replacing the dream as a whole by another whole to which it stands in a symbolic relation. Serious-minded people smile at these efforts: '*Träume sind Schäume*' – 'dreams are froth'.

II

One day I discovered to my great astonishment that the view of dreams which came nearest to the truth was not the medical but the popular one, half involved though it still was in superstition. For I had been led to fresh conclusions on the subject of dreams by applying to them a new method of psychological investigation which had done excellent service in the solution of phobias, obsessions and delusions, etc. Since then, under the name of 'psycho-analysis', it has found acceptance by a whole school of research workers. The numerous analogies that exist between dream-life and a great variety of conditions of psychical illness in waking life have indeed been correctly observed by many medical investigators. There seemed, therefore, good ground for hoping that a method of investigation which had given satisfactory results in the case of psychopathic structures would also be of use in throwing light upon dreams. Phobias and obsessions are as alien to normal consciousness as dreams are to waking consciousness; their origin is as unknown to consciousness as that of dreams. In the case of these psychopathic structures practical considerations led to an investigation of their origin and mode of development; for experience had shown that the discovery of the trains of thought which, concealed from consciousness, connect the pathological ideas with the remaining contents of the mind is equivalent to a resolution of the symptoms and has as its consequence the mastering of ideas which till then could not be inhibited. Thus psychotherapy was the starting-point of the procedure of which I made use for the explanation of dreams.

This procedure is easily described, although instruction and practice would be necessary before it could be put into effect.

If we make use of it on someone else, let us say on a patient with a phobia, we require him to direct his attention on to the idea in question, not, however, to reflect upon it as he has done so often already, but to take notice of *whatever occurs to his mind without any exception* and report it to the physician. If he should then assert that his attention is unable to grasp anything at all, we dismiss this with an energetic assurance that a complete absence of any ideational subject-matter is quite impossible. And in fact very soon numerous ideas will occur to him and will lead on to others; but they will invariably be prefaced by a judgement on the part of the self-observer to the effect that they are senseless or unimportant, that they are irrelevant, and that they occurred to him by chance and without any connection with the topic under consideration. We perceive at once that it was this critical attitude which prevented the subject from reporting any of these ideas, and which indeed had previously prevented them from becoming conscious. If we can induce him to abandon his criticism of the ideas that occur to him, and to continue pursuing the trains of thought which will emerge so long as he keeps his attention turned upon them; we find ourselves in possession of a quantity of psychical material, which we soon find is clearly connected with the pathological idea which was our starting-point; this material will soon reveal connections between the pathological idea and other ideas, and will eventually enable us to replace the pathological idea by a new one which fits into the nexus of thought in an intelligible fashion.

This is not the place in which to give a detailed account of the premises upon which this experiment was based, or the consequences which follow from its invariable success. It will therefore be enough to say that we obtain material that enables us to resolve any pathological idea if we turn our attention precisely to those associations which are 'involuntary', which 'interfere with our reflection', and which are normally dismissed by our critical faculty as worthless rubbish.

If we make use of this procedure upon *ourselves*, we can best assist the investigation by at once writing down what are at first unintelligible associations.

I will now show what results follow if I apply this method of investigation to dreams. Any example of a dream should in fact be equally appropriate for the purpose; but for particular reasons I will choose some dream of my own, one which seems obscure and meaningless as I remember it, and one which has the advantage of brevity. A dream which I actually had last night will perhaps meet these requirements. Its content, as I noted it down immediately after waking up, was as follows:

'Company at table or table d'hôte . . . spinach was being eaten . . . Frau E. L. was sitting beside me; she was turning her whole attention to me and laid her hand on my knee in an intimate manner. I removed her hand unresponsively. She then said: "But you've always had such beautiful eyes." . . . I then had an indistinct picture of two eyes, as though it were a drawing or like the outline of a pair of spectacles . . .'

This was the whole of the dream, or at least all that I could remember of it. It seemed to me obscure and meaningless, but above all surprising. Frau E. L. is a person with whom I have hardly at any time been on friendly terms, nor, so far as I know, have I ever wished to have any closer relations with her. I have not seen her for a long time, and her name has not, I believe, been mentioned during the last few days. The dream-process was not accompanied by affects of any kind.

Reflecting over this dream brought me no nearer to understanding it. I determined, however, to set down without any premeditation or criticism the associations which presented themselves to my self-observation. As I have found, it is advisable for this purpose to divide a dream into its elements and to find the associations attaching to each of these fragments separately.

Company at table or table d'hôte. This at once reminded me of an episode which occurred late yesterday evening. I came away from a small party in the company of a friend who offered to take a cab and drive me home in it. 'I prefer taking a cab with a taximeter,' he said, 'it occupies one's mind so agreeably; one always has something to look at.' When we had taken our places in the cab and the driver had set the dial, so that the first charge of sixty hellers became visible, I carried the joke further. 'We've only just got in,' I said, 'and already we owe him sixty hellers. A cab with a taximeter always reminds me of a table d'hôte. It makes me avaricious and selfish, because it keeps on reminding me of what I owe. My debt seems to be growing too fast, and I'm afraid of getting the worst of the bargain; and in just the same way at a table d'hôte I can't avoid feeling in a comic way that I'm getting too little, and must keep an eye on my own interests.' I went on to quote, somewhat discursively:

Ihr führt ins Leben uns hinein,

Ihr lasst den Armen *schuldig* werden.[2]

And now a second association to 'table d'hôte'. A few weeks ago, while we were at table in a hotel at a mountain resort in the Tyrol, I was very much annoyed because I thought my wife was not being sufficiently reserved towards some people sitting near us whose acquaintance I had no desire at all to make. I asked her to concern herself more with me than with these strangers. This was again *as thought I were getting the worst of the bargain at the table d'hôte*. I was struck too by the contrast between my wife's behaviour at table and that of Frau E. L. in the dream, who 'turned her whole attention to me'.

To proceed. I now saw that the events in the dream were a reproduction of a small episode of a precisely similar kind which occurred between my wife and me at the time at which I was secretly courting her. The caress which she gave me under the table-cloth was her reply to a pressing love letter. In the dream, however, my wife was replaced by a comparative stranger – E. L.

Frau E. L. is the daughter of a man to whom I was once *in debt*. I could not help noticing that this revealed an unsuspected connection between parts of the content of the dream and my associations. If one follows the train of association starting out from one element of a dream's content, one is soon brought back to another of its elements. My associations to the dream were bringing to light connections which were not visible in the dream itself.

If a person expects one to keep an eye on his interests without any advantage to oneself, his artlessness is apt to provoke the scornful question: 'Do you suppose I'm going to do this or that for the sake of your *beaux yeux* [*beautiful eyes*]?' That being so, Frau E. L.'s speech in the dream, 'You've always had such beautiful eyes', can only have meant: 'People have always done everything for you for love; you have always had everything *without paying for it*.' The truth is, of course, just the contrary: I have always paid dearly for whatever advantage I have had from other people. The fact that my friend took me home yesterday in a cab *without my paying for it* must, after all, have made an impression on me.

Incidentally, the friend whose guests we were yesterday has often put me in his debt. Only recently I allowed an opportunity of repaying him to slip by. He has had only one present from me – an antique bowl, round which there are *eyes* painted: what is known as an *'occhiale'*, to avert the *evil eye*. Moreover he is an *eye surgeon*. The same evening I asked him after a woman patient, whom I had sent on to him for a consultation to fit her with *spectacles*.

As I now perceived, almost all the elements of the dream's content had been brought into the new context. For the sake of consistency, however, the further question might be asked of why *spinach*, of all things, was being served in the dream. The answer was that *spinach* reminded me of an episode which occurred not long ago at our family table, when one of the children – and precisely the one who really deserves to be admired for his *beautiful eyes* – refused to eat any spinach. I myself behaved in just the same way when I was a child; for a long time I detested spinach, till eventually my taste changed and promoted that vegetable into one of my favourite foods. My own early life and my child's were thus brought together by the mention of this dish. 'You ought to be glad to have spinach,' the little *gourmet*'s mother exclaimed; 'there are children who would be only too pleased to have spinach.' Thus I was reminded of the duties of parents to their children. Goethe's words

> Ihr führt ins Leben uns hinein,
> Ihr lasst den Armen schuldig werden

gained a fresh meaning in this connection.[3]

I will pause here to survey the results I had so far reached in my dream-analysis. By following the associations which arose from the separate elements of the dream divorced from their context, I arrived at a number of thoughts and recollections, which I could not fail to recognize as important products of my mental life. This material revealed by the analysis of the dream was intimately connected with the dream's content, yet the connection was of such a kind that I could never have inferred the fresh material from that content. The dream was unemotional, disconnected and unintelligible; but while I was producing the thoughts behind the dream, I was aware of intense and well-founded affective impulses; the thoughts themselves fell at once into logical chains, in which certain ideas made their appearance more than once. Thus, the contrast between 'selfish' and 'unselfish', and the elements 'being in debt' and 'without paying for it' were central ideas of this kind, not represented in the dream itself. I might draw closer together the threads in the material revealed by the analysis, and I might then show that they converge upon a single nodal point, but considerations of a personal and not of a scientific nature prevent my doing so in public. I should be obliged to betray many things which had better remain my secret, for on my way to discovering the solution of the dream all kinds of things were revealed which I was unwilling to admit even to myself. Why then, it will be asked, have I not chosen some other dream, whose analysis is better suited for reporting, so that I could produce more convincing evidence of the meaning and connectedness of the material uncovered by analysis? The answer is that *every* dream with which I might try to deal would lead to things equally hard to report and would impose an equal discretion upon me. Nor should I avoid this difficulty by bringing up someone else's dream for analysis, unless circumstances enabled me to drop all disguise without damage to the person who had confided in me.

At the point which I have now reached, I am led to regard the dream as a sort of *substitute* for the thought-processes, full of meaning and emotion, at which I arrived after the completion of the analysis. We do not yet know the nature of the process which has caused the dream to be generated from these thoughts, but we can see that it is wrong to regard it as purely physical and without psychical meaning, as a process which has arisen from the isolated activity of separate groups of brain cells aroused from sleep.

Two other things are already clear. The content of the dream is very much shorter than the thoughts for which I regard it as a substitute; and analysis has revealed that the instigator of the dream was an unimportant event of the evening before I dreamt it.

I should, of course, not draw such far-reaching conclusions if only a single dream-analysis was at my disposal. If experience shows me, however, that by uncritically pursuing the associations arising from *any* dream I can arrive at a similar train of thoughts, among the elements of which the constituents of the dream re-appear and which are interconnected in a rational and intelligible manner, then it will be safe to disregard the slight possibility that the connections observed in a first experiment might be due to chance. I think I am justified, therefore, in adopting a terminology which will crystallize our new discovery. In order to contrast the dream as it is retained in my memory with the relevant material discovered by analysing it, I shall speak of the former as the '*manifest* content of the dream' and the latter – without, in the first instance, making any further distinction – as the '*latent* content of the dream'. I am now faced by two new problems which have not hitherto been formulated. (1) What is the psychical process which has transformed the latent content of the dream into the manifest one which is known to me from my memory? (2) What are the motive or motives which have necessitated this transformation? I shall describe the process which transforms the latent into the manifest content of dreams as the 'dream-work'. The counterpart to this activity – one which brings about a transformation in the opposite direction – is already known to us as the work of analysis. The remaining problems arising out of dreams – questions as to the instigators of dreams, as to the origin of their material, as to their possible meaning, as to the possible function of dreaming, and as to the reasons for dreams being forgotten – all these problems will be discussed by me on the basis, not of the manifest, but of the newly discovered latent dream-content. Since I attribute all the contradictory and incorrect views upon dream-life which appear in the literature of the subject to ignorance of the latent content of dreams as revealed by analysis, I shall be at the greatest pains henceforward to avoid confusing the *manifest dream* with the *latent dream-thoughts*.

III

The transformation of the latent dream-thoughts into the manifest dream-content deserves all our attention, since it is the first instance known to us of psychical material being changed over from one mode of expression to another, from a mode of expression which is immediately intelligible to us to another which we can only come to understand with the help of guidance and effort, though it too must be recognized as a function of our mental activity.

Dreams can be divided into three categories in respect of the relation between their latent and manifest content. In the first place, we may distinguish those dreams which *make sense* and are at the same time *intelligible*, which, that is to say, can be inserted without further difficulty into the context of our mental life. We have numbers of such dreams. They are for the most part short and appear to us in general to deserve little attention, since there is nothing astonishing or strange about them. Incidentally, their occurrence constitutes a powerful argument against the theory according to which dreams originate from the isolated activity of separate groups of brain cells. They give no indication of reduced or fragmentary psychical activity, but nevertheless we never question the fact of their being dreams, and do not confuse them with the products of waking life. A second group is formed by those dreams which, though they are connected in themselves and have a clear sense, nevertheless have a *bewildering* effect, because we cannot see how to fit that sense into our mental life. Such would be the case if we were to dream, for instance, that a relative of whom we were fond had died of the plague, when we had no reason for expecting, fearing or assuming any such thing; we should ask in astonishment: 'How did I get hold of such an idea?' The third group, finally, contains those dreams which are without either sense or intelligibility, which seem *disconnected*, *confused* and *meaningless*. The preponderant majority of the products of our dreaming exhibit these characteristics, which are the basis of the low opinion in which dreams are held and of the medical theory that they are the outcome of a restricted mental activity. The most evident signs of incoherence are seldom absent, especially in dream-compositions of any considerable length and complexity.

The contrast between the manifest and latent content of dreams is clearly of significance only for dreams of the second and more particularly of the third category. It is there that we are faced by riddles which only disappear after we have replaced the manifest dream by the latent thoughts behind it; and it was on a specimen of the last category – a confused and unintelligible dream – that the analysis which I have just recorded was carried out. Contrary to our expectation, however, we came up against motives which prevented us from becoming fully acquainted with the latent dream-thoughts. A repetition of similar experiences may lead us to suspect that *there is an intimate and regular relation between the unintelligible and confused nature of dreams and the difficulty of reporting the thoughts behind them.* Before enquiring into the nature of this relation, we may with advantage turn our attention to the more easily intelligible dreams of the first category, in which the manifest and latent content coincide, and there appears to be a consequent saving in dream-work.

Moreover, an examination of these dreams offers advantages from another standpoint. For *children's* dreams are of that kind – significant and not puzzling. Here, incidentally, we have a further argument against tracing the origin of dreams to dissociated cerebral activity during sleep. For why should a reduction in psychical functioning of this kind be a characteristic of the state of sleep in the case of adults but not in that of children? On the other hand, we shall be fully justified in expecting that an explanation of psychical processes in children, in whom they may well be greatly simplified, may turn out to be an indispensable prelude to the investigation of the psychology of adults.

I will therefore record a few instances of dreams which I have collected from children. A little girl nineteen months old had been kept without food all day because she had had an attack of vomiting in the morning; her nurse declared that she had been upset by eating strawberries. During the night after this day of starvation she was heard saying her own name in her sleep and adding: '*Stwawbewwies, wild stwawbewwies, omblet, pudden!*' She was thus dreaming of eating a meal, and she laid special stress in her menu on the particular delicacy of which, as she had reason to expect, she would only be allowed scanty quantities in the near future. – A little boy of twenty-two months had a similar dream of a feast which he had been denied. The day before, he had been obliged to present his uncle with a gift of a basket of fresh cherries, of which he himself, of course, had only been allowed to taste a single sample. He awoke with this cheerful news: '*Hermann eaten all the chewwies!*' – One day a girl of three and a quarter made a trip across a lake. The voyage was evidently not long enough for her, for she cried when she had to get off the boat. Next morning she reported that during the night she had been for a trip on the lake: she had been continuing her interrupted voyage. – A boy of five and a quarter showed signs of dissatisfaction in the course of a walk in the neighbourhood of the Dachstein. Each time a new mountain came into view he asked if it was the Dachstein and finally refused to visit a waterfall with the rest of the company. His behaviour was attributed to fatigue; but it found a better explanation when next morning he reported that he had dreamt that *he had climbed up the Dachstein*. He had evidently had the idea that the expedition would end in a climb up the Dachstein, and had become depressed when the promised mountain never came in view. He made up in his dream for what the previous day had failed to give him. – A six-year-old girl had an exactly similar dream. In the course of a walk her father had stopped short of their intended goal as the hour was getting late. On their way back she had noticed a signpost bearing the name of another landmark; and her father had promised to take her there as well another time. Next morning she met her father with the news that she had dreamt that *he had been with her to both places*.

The common element in all these children's dreams is obvious. All of them fulfilled wishes which were active during the day but had remained unfulfilled. The dreams were simple and undisguised *wish-fulfilments*.

Here is another child's dream, which, though at first sight it is not quite easy to understand, is also nothing more than a wish-fulfilment. A little girl not quite four years old had been brought to town from the country because she was suffering from an attack of poliomyelitis. She spent the night with an aunt who had no children, and was put to sleep in a large bed – much too large for her, of course. Next morning she said she had had a dream that *the bed had been far too small for her, and that there had been no room for her in it*. It is easy to recognize this dream as a wishful dream if we remember that children very often express a wish '*to be big*'. The size of the bed was a disagreeable reminder of her smallness to the would-be big child; she therefore corrected the unwelcome relation in her dream, and grew so big that even the large bed was too small for her.

Even when the content of children's dreams becomes complicated and subtle, there is never any difficulty in recognizing them as wish-fulfilments. An eight-year-old boy had a dream that he was driving in a chariot with Achilles and that Diomede was the charioteer. It was shown that the day before he had been deep in a book of legends about the Greek heroes; and it was easy to see that he had taken the heroes as his models and was sorry not to be living in their days.[4]

This small collection throws a direct light on a further characteristic of children's dreams: their connection with daytime life. The wishes which are fulfilled in them are carried over from daytime and as a rule from the day before, and in waking life they have been accompanied by intense emotion. Nothing unimportant or indifferent, or nothing which would strike a child as such, finds its way into the content of their dreams.

Numerous examples of dreams of this infantile type can be found occurring in adults as well, though, as I have said, they are usually brief in content. Thus a number of people regularly respond to a stimulus of thirst during the night with dreams of drinking, which thus endeavour to get rid of the stimulus and enable sleep to continue. In some people 'dreams of convenience' of this kind often occur before waking, when the necessity for getting up presents itself. They dream that they are already up and at the washing-stand, or that they are already at the school or office where they are due at some particular time.

During the night before a journey we not infrequently dream of having arrived at our destination; so too, before a visit to the theatre or a party, a dream will often anticipate the pleasure that lies ahead – out of impatience, as it were. In other dreams the wish-fulfilment is expressed a stage more indirectly: some connection or implication must be established – that is, the work of interpretation must be begun – before the wish-fulfilment can be recognized. A man told me, for instance, that his young wife had had a dream that her period had started. I reflected that if this young woman had missed her period she must have known that she was faced with a pregnancy. Thus when she reported her dream she was announcing her pregnancy, and the meaning of the dream was to represent as fulfilled her wish that the pregnancy might be postponed for a while. Under unusual or extreme conditions dreams of this infantile character are particularly common. Thus the leader of a polar expedition has recorded that the members of his expedition, while they were wintering in the ice-field and living on a monotonous diet and short rations, regularly dreamt like children of large meals, of mountains of tobacco, and of being back at home.

It by no means rarely happens that in the course of a comparatively long, complicated and on the whole confused dream one particularly clear portion stands out, which contains an unmistakable wish-fulfilment, but which is bound up with some other, unintelligible material. But in the case of adults, anyone with some experience in analysing their dreams will find to his surprise that even those dreams which have an appearance of being transparently clear are seldom as simple as those of children, and that behind the obvious wish-fulfilment some other meaning may lie concealed.

It would indeed be a simple and satisfactory solution of the riddle of dreams if the work of analysis were to enable us to trace even the meaningless and confused dreams of adults back to the infantile type of fulfilment of an intensely felt wish of the previous day. There can be no doubt, however, that appearances do not speak in favour of such an expectation. Dreams are usually full of the most indifferent and strangest material, and there is no sign in their content of the fulfilment of any wish.

But before taking leave of infantile dreams with their undisguised wish-fulfilments, I must not omit to mention one principal feature of dreams, which has long been evident and which emerges particularly clearly precisely in this group. Every one of these dreams can be replaced by an optative clause: 'Oh, if only the trip on the lake had lasted longer!' – 'If only I were already washed and dressed!' – 'If only I could have kept the cherries instead of giving them to Uncle!' But dreams give us more than such optative clauses. They show us the wish as already fulfilled; they represent its fulfilment as real and present; and the material employed in dream-representation consists principally, though not exclusively, of situations and

Dreams are usually full of the most indifferent and strangest material, and there is no sign in their content of the fulfilment of any wish

of sensory images, mostly of a visual character. Thus, even in this infantile group, a species of transformation, which deserves to be described as dream-work, is not completely absent: *a thought expressed in the optative has been replaced by a representation in the present tense.*

IV

We shall be inclined to suppose that a transformation of some such kind has occurred even in confused dreams, though we cannot tell whether what has been transformed was an optative in their case too. There are, however, two passages in the specimen dream which I have reported, and with whose analysis we have made some headway, that give us reason to suspect something of the kind. The analysis showed that my wife had concerned herself with some other people at table, and that I had found this disagreeable; the dream contained precisely the opposite of this – the person who took the place of my wife was turning her whole attention to me. But a disagreeable experience can give rise to no more suitable wish than that its opposite might have occurred – which was what the dream represented as fulfilled. There was an exactly similar relation between the bitter thought revealed in the analysis that I had never had anything free of cost and the remark made by the woman in the dream – 'You've always had such beautiful eyes.' Some part of the opposition between the manifest and latent content of dreams is thus attributable to wish-fulfilment.

But another achievement of the dream-work, tending as it does to produce incoherent dreams, is even more striking. If in any particular instance we compare the number of ideational elements or the space taken up in writing them down in the case of the dream and of the dream-thoughts to which the analysis leads us and of which traces are to be found in the dream itself, we shall be left in no doubt that the dream-work has carried out a work of compression or *condensation* on a large scale. It is impossible at first to form any judgement of the degree of this condensation; but the deeper we plunge into a dream-analysis the more impressive it seems. From every element in a dream's content associative threads branch out in two or more directions; every situation in a dream seems to be put together out of two or more impressions or experiences. For instance, I once had a dream of a sort of swimming-pool, in which the bathers were scattering in all directions; at one point on the edge of the pool someone was standing and bending towards one of the people bathing, as though to help her out of the water. The situation was put together from a memory of an experience I had had at puberty and from two paintings, one of which I had seen shortly before the dream. One was a picture from Schwind's series illustrating the legend of Mélusine, which showed the water-nymphs surprised in their pool (cf. the scattering bathers in the dream); the other was a picture of the Deluge by an Italian Master; while the little experience remembered from my puberty was of having seen the instructor at a swimming-school helping a lady out of the water who had stopped in until after the time set aside for men bathers. – In the case of the example which I chose for interpretation, an analysis of the situation led me to a small series of recollections each of which contributed something to the content of the dream. In the first place, there was the episode from the time of my engagement of which I have already spoken. The pressure upon my hand under the table, which was a part of that episode, provided the dream with the detail 'under the table' – a detail which I had to add as an after-thought to my memory of the dream. In the episode itself there was of course no question of 'turning to me'; the analysis showed that this element was the fulfilment of a wish by presenting the opposite of an actual event, and that it related to my wife's behaviour at the table d'hôte. But behind this recent recollection there lay concealed an exactly similar and far more important scene from the time of our engagement, which estranged us for a whole day: The intimate laying of a hand on my knee belonged to a quite different context and was concerned with quite other people. This element in the dream was in turn the starting-point of two separate sets of memories – and so on.

The material in the dream-thoughts which is packed together for the purpose of constructing a dream-situation must of course in itself be adaptable for that purpose. There must be one or more *common elements* in all the components. The dream-work then proceeds just as Francis Galton did in constructing his family photographs. It superimposes, as it were, the different components upon one another. The common element in them then stands out clearly in the composite picture, while contradictory details more or less wipe one another out. This method of production also explains to some extent the varying degrees of characteristic vagueness shown by so many elements in the content of dreams. Basing itself on this discovery, dream-interpretation has laid down the following rule: in analysing a dream, if an uncertainty can be resolved into an 'either–or', we must replace it for purposes of interpretation by an 'and', and take each of the apparent alternatives as an independent starting-point for a series of associations.

If a common element of this kind between the dream-thoughts is not present, the dream-work sets about *creating* one, so that it may be possible for the thoughts to be given a common representation in the dream. The most convenient way of bringing together two dream-thoughts which, to start with, have nothing in common, is to alter the verbal form of one of them, and thus bring it half-way to meet the other, which may be similarly clothed in a new form of words. A parallel process is involved in hammering out a rhyme, where a similar sound has to be sought for in the same way as a common element is in our present case. A large part of the dream-work consists in the creation of intermediate thoughts of this kind which are often highly ingenious, though they frequently appear far-fetched; these then form a link between the composite picture in the manifest content of the dream and the dream-thoughts, which are themselves diverse both in form and essence and have been determined by the exciting factors of the dream. The analysis of our sample dream affords us an instance of this kind in which a thought has been given a new form in order to bring it into contact with another which is essentially foreign to it. In carrying out the analysis I came upon the following thought: '*I should like to get something sometimes without paying for it.*' But in that form the thought could not be employed in the dream-content. It was therefore given a fresh form: '*I should like to get some enjoyment without cost* ["Kosten"].'[5] Now the word '*Kosten*' in its second sense fits into the 'table d'hôte' circle of ideas, and could thus be represented in the '*spinach*' which was served in the dream. When a dish appears at our table and the children refuse it, their mother begins by trying persuasion, and urges them '*just to taste* ["*kosten*"] *a bit of it*'. It may seem strange that the dream-work should make such free use of verbal ambiguity, but further experience will teach us that the occurrence is quite a common one.

The process of condensation further explains certain constituents of the content of dreams which are peculiar to them and are not found in waking ideation. What I have in mind are 'collective' and 'composite figures' and the strange 'composite structures', which are creations not unlike the composite animals invented by the folk-imagination of the Orient. The latter, however, have already assumed stereotyped shapes in our thought, whereas in dreams fresh composite forms are being perpetually constructed in an inexhaustible variety. We are all of us familiar with such structures from our own dreams.

There are many sorts of ways in which figures of this kind can be put together. I may build up a figure by giving it the features of two people; or I may give it the *form* of one person but think of it in the dream as having the *name* of another person; or I may have a visual picture of one person, but put it in a situation which is appropriate to another. In all these cases the combination of different persons into a single representative in the content of the dream has a meaning; it is intended to indicate an 'and' or 'just as', or to compare the original persons with each other in some particular respect, which may even be specified in the dream itself. As a rule, however, this common element between the combined persons can only be discovered by analysis, and is only indicated in the contents of the dream by the formation of the collective figure.

The composite structures which occur in dreams in such immense numbers are put together in an equal variety of ways, and the same rules apply to their resolution. There is no need for me to quote any instances. Their strangeness disappears completely when once we have made up our minds not to class them with the objects of our waking perception, but to remember that they are products of dream-condensation and are emphasizing in an effectively abbreviated form some common characteristic of the objects which they are thus combining. Here again the common element has as a rule to be discovered by analysis. The content of the dream merely says as it were: 'All these things have an element x in common.' The dissection of these composite structures by means of analysis is often the shortest way to finding the meaning of a dream. – Thus, I dreamt on one occasion that I was sitting on a bench with one of my former university teachers, and that the bench, which was surrounded by other benches, was moving forward at a rapid pace. This was a combination of a lecture theatre and a *trottoir roulant*.[6] I will not pursue this train of ideas further. – Another time I was sitting in a railway carriage and holding on my lap an object in the shape of a top-hat ['*Zylinderhut*', literally 'cylinder-hat'], which however was made of transparent glass. The situation made me think at once of the proverb: '*Mit dem Hute in der Hand kommt man durchs ganze Land.*'[7] The glass cylinder led me by a short *détour* to think of an incandescent gas-mantle; and I soon saw that I should like to make a discovery which would make me as rich and independent as my fellow-countryman Dr Auer von Welsbach was made by his, and that I should like to travel instead of stopping in Vienna. In the dream I was travelling with my discovery, the hat in the shape of a glass cylinder – a discovery which, it is true, was not as yet of any great practical use. – The dream-work is particularly fond of representing two *contrary* ideas by the same composite structure. Thus, for instance, a woman had a dream in which she saw herself carrying a tall spray of flowers, such as the angel is represented as holding in pictures of the Annunciation. (This stood for innocence; incidentally, her own name was Maria.) On the other hand, the spray was covered with large white[8] flowers like camellias. (This stood for the opposite of innocence; it was associated with *La dame aux camélias*.)

A good proportion of what we have learnt about condensation in dreams may be summarized in this formula: each element in the content of a dream is 'overdetermined' by material in the dream-thoughts; it is not derived from a *single* element in the dream-thoughts, but may be traced back to a whole number. These elements need not necessarily be closely related to each other in the dream-thoughts themselves; they may belong to the most widely separated regions of the fabric of those thoughts. A dream-element is, in the strictest sense of the word, the 'representative' of all this disparate material in the content of the dream. But analysis reveals yet another side of the complicated relation between the content of the dream and the dream-thoughts. Just as connections lead from each element of the dream to several dream-thoughts, so as a rule a single dream-thought is represented by more than one dream-element; the threads of association do not simply converge from the dream-thoughts to the dream-content, they cross and interweave with each other many times over in the course of their journey.

Condensation, together with the transformation of thoughts into situations ('dramatization'), is the most important and peculiar characteristic of the dream-work. So far, however, nothing has transpired as to any *motive* necessitating this compression of the material.

V

In the case of the complicated and confused dreams with which we are now concerned, condensation and dramatization alone are not enough to account for the whole of the impression that we gain of the dissimilarity between the content of the dream and the dream-thoughts. We have evidence of the operation of a third factor, and this evidence deserves careful sifting.

First and foremost, when by means of analysis we have arrived at a knowledge of the dream-thoughts, we observe that the manifest dream-content deals with quite different material from the latent thoughts. This, to be sure, is no more than an appearance, which evaporates under closer examination, for we find ultimately that the whole of the dream-content is derived from the dream-thoughts, and that almost all the dream-throughts are represented in the dream-content. Nevertheless, something of the distinction still remains. What stands out boldly and clearly in the dream as its essential content must, after analysis, be satisfied with playing an extremely subordinate role among the dream-thoughts; and what, on the evidence of our feelings, can claim to be the most prominent among the dream-thoughts is either not present at all as ideational material in the content of the dream or is only remotely alluded to in some obscure region of it. We may put it in this way: *in the course of the dream-work the psychical intensity passes over from the thoughts and ideas to which it properly belongs on to others which in our judgement have no claim to any such emphasis*. No other process contributes so much to concealing the meaning of a dream and to making the connection between the dream-content and the dream-thoughts unrecognizable. In the course of this process, which I shall describe as 'dream-displacement', the psychical intensity, significance or affective potentiality of the thoughts is, as we further find, transformed into sensory vividness. We assume as a matter of course that the most distinct element in the manifest content of a dream is the most important one; but in fact [owing to the displacement that has occurred] it is often an *indistinct* element which turns out to be the most direct derivative of the essential dream-thought.

What I have called dream-displacement might equally be described [in Nietzsche's phrase] as 'a transvaluation of psychical values'. I shall not have given an exhaustive estimate of this phenomenon, however, unless I add that this work of displacement or transvaluation is performed to a very varying degree in different dreams. There are dreams which come about almost without any displacement. These are the ones which make sense and are intelligible, such, for instance, as those which we have recognized as undisguised wishful dreams. On the other hand, there are dreams in which not a single piece of the dream-thoughts has retained its own psychical value, or in which everything that is essential in the dream-thoughts has been replaced by something trivial. And we can find a complete series of transitional cases between these two extremes. The more obscure and confused a dream appears to be, the greater the share in its construction which may be attributed to the factor of displacement.

Our specimen dream exhibits displacement to this extent at least, that its content seems to have a different *centre* from its dream-thoughts. In the foreground of the dream-content a prominent place is taken by a situation in which a woman seems to be making advances to me; while in the dream-thoughts the chief emphasis is laid on a wish for once to enjoy unselfish love, love which 'costs nothing' – an idea concealed behind the phrase about 'beautiful eyes' and the far-fetched allusion to 'spinach'.

If we undo dream-displacement by means of analysis, we obtain what seems to be completely trustworthy information on two much-disputed problems concerning dreams: as to their instigators and as to their connection with waking life. There are dreams which immediately reveal their derivation from events of the day; there are others in which no trace of any such derivation is to be discovered. If we seek the help of analysis, we find that every dream without any possible exception goes back to an impression of the past few days, or, it is probably more correct to say, of the day immediately preceding the dream, of the 'dream-day'. The impression which plays the part of dream-instigator may be such an important one that we feel no surprise at being concerned with it in the daytime, and in that case we rightly speak of the dream as carrying on with the significant interests of our waking life. As a rule, however, if a connection is to be found in the content of the dream with any impression of the previous day, that impression is so trivial, insignificant and unmemorable, that it is only with difficulty that we ourselves can recall it. And in such cases the content of the dream itself, even if it is connected and intelligible, seems to be concerned with the most indifferent trivialities, which would be unworthy of our interest if we were awake. A good deal of the contempt in which dreams are held is due to the preference thus shown in their content for what is indifferent and trivial.

Analysis does away with the misleading appearance upon which this derogatory judgement is founded. If the content of a dream puts forward some indifferent impression as being its instigator, analysis invariably brings to light a significant experience, and one by which the dreamer has good reason to be stirred. This experience has been replaced by the indifferent one, with which it is connected by copious associative links. Where the content of the dream treats of insignificant and uninteresting ideational material, analysis uncovers the numerous associative paths connecting these trivialities with things that are of the highest psychical importance in the dreamer's estimation. *If what make their way into the content of dreams are impressions and material which are indifferent and trivial rather than justifiably stirring and interesting, that is only the effect of the process of displacement.* If we answer our questions about dream-instigators and the connection between dreaming and daily affairs on the basis of the new insight we have gained from replacing the manifest by the latent content of dreams, we arrive at these conclusions: *dreams are never concerned with things which we should not think it worth while to be concerned with during the day, and trivialities which do not affect us during the day are unable to pursue us in our sleep.*

What was the dream-instigator in the specimen that we have chosen for analysis? It was the definitely insignificant event of my friend giving me *a drive in a cab free of cost*. The situation in the dream at the table d'hôte contained an allusion to this insignificant precipitating cause, for in my conversation I had compared the taximeter cab with a table d'hôte. But I can also point to the important experience which was represented by this trivial one. A few days earlier I had paid out a considerable sum of money on behalf of a member of my family of whom I am fond. No wonder, said the dream-thoughts, if this person were to feel grateful to me: love of that sort would not be 'free of cost'. Love that is free of cost, however, stood in the forefront of the dream-thoughts. The fact that not long before I had had several *cab-drives* with the relative in question, made it possible for the cab-drive with my friend to remind me of my connections with this other person.

The indifferent impression which becomes a dream-instigator owing to associations of this kind is subject to a further condition which does not apply to the true source of the dream: it must always be a *recent* impression, derived from the dream-day.

I cannot leave the subject of dream-displacement without drawing attention to a remarkable process which occurs in the formation of dreams and in which condensation and displacement *combine* to produce the result. In considering condensation we have already seen the way in which two ideas in the dream-thoughts which have something in common, some point of contact, are replaced in the dream-content by a composite idea, in which a relatively distinct nucleus represents what they have in common, while indistinct subordinate details correspond to the respects in which they differ from each other. If displacement takes place in addition to condensation, what is constructed is not a composite idea but an 'intermediate common entity', which stands in a relation to the two different elements similar to that in which the resultant in a parallelogram of forces stands to its components. For instance, in the content of one of my dreams there was a question of an injection with *propyl*. To begin with, the analysis only led me to an indifferent experience which had acted as dream-instigator, and in which a part was played by *amyl*. I was not yet able to justify the confusion between amyl and propyl. In the group of ideas behind this same dream, however, there was also a recollection of my first visit to Munich, where I had been struck by the *Propylaea*.[9] The details of the analysis made it plausible to suppose that it was the influence of this second group of ideas upon the first one that was responsible for the displacement from amyl to propyl. *Propyl* is as it were an intermediate idea between *amyl* and *Propylaea*, and found its way into the content of the dream as a kind of *compromise*, by means of simultaneous condensation and displacement.

There is a still more urgent necessity in the case of the process of displacement than in that of condensation to discover the motive for these puzzling efforts on the part of the dream-work.

VI

It is the process of displacement which is chiefly responsible for our being unable to discover or recognize the dream-thoughts in the dream-content, unless we understand the reason for their distortion. Nevertheless, the dream-thoughts are also submitted to another and milder sort of transformation, which leads to our discovering a new achievement on the part of the dream-work – one, however, which is easily intelligible. The dream-thoughts which we first come across as we proceed with our analysis often strike us by the unusual form in which they are expressed; they are not clothed in the prosaic language usually employed by our thoughts, but are on the contrary represented symbolically by means of similes and metaphors, in images resembling those of poetic speech. There is no difficulty in accounting for the constraint imposed upon the form in which the dream-thoughts are expressed. The manifest content of dreams consists for the most part in pictorial situations; and the dream-thoughts must accordingly be submitted in the first place to a treatment which will make them suitable for a representation of this kind. If we imagine ourselves faced by the problem of representing the arguments in a political leading article or the speeches of counsel before a court of law in a series of pictures, we shall easily understand the modifications which must necessarily be carried out by the dream-work owing to *considerations of representability in the content of the dream.*

The psychical material of the dream-thoughts habitually includes recollections of impressive experiences – not infrequently dating back to early childhood – which are thus themselves perceived as a rule as situations having a visual subject-matter. Wherever the possibility arises, this portion of the dream-thoughts exercises a determining influence upon the form taken by the content of the dream; it constitutes, as it were, a nucleus of crystallization, attracting the material of the dream-thoughts to itself and thus affecting their distribution. The situation in a dream is often nothing other than a modified repetition, complicated by interpolations, of an impressive experience of this kind; on the other hand, faithful and straightforward reproductions of real scenes only rarely appear in dreams.

The content of dreams, however, does not consist entirely of situations, but also includes disconnected fragments of visual images, speeches and even bits of unmodified thoughts. It may therefore perhaps be of interest to enumerate very briefly the modes of representation available to the dream-work for reproducing the dream-thoughts in the peculiar form of expression necessary in dreams.

The dream-thoughts which we arrive at by means of analysis reveal themselves as a psychical complex of the most intricate possible structure. Its portions stand in the most manifold logical relations to one another: they represent foreground and background, conditions, digressions and illustrations, chains of evidence and counter-arguments. Each train of thought is almost invariably accompanied by its contradictory counterpart. This material lacks none of the characteristics that are familiar to us from our waking thinking. If now all of this is to be turned into a dream, the psychical material will be submitted to a pressure which will condense it greatly, to an internal fragmentation and displacement which will, as it were, create new surfaces, and to a selective operation in favour of those portions of it which are the most appropriate for the construction of situations. If we take into account the genesis of the material, a process of this sort deserves to be described as a 'regression'. In the course of this transformation, however, the logical links which have hitherto held the psychical material together are lost. It is only, as it were, the substantive content of the dream-thoughts that the dream-work takes over and manipulates. The restoration of the connections which the dream-work has destroyed is a task which has to be performed by the work of analysis.

The modes of expression open to a dream may therefore be qualified as meagre by comparison with those of our intellectual speech; nevertheless a dream need not wholly abandon the possibility of reproducing the logical relations present in the dream-thoughts. On the contrary, it succeeds often enough in replacing them by formal characteristics in its own texture.

In the first place, dreams take into account the connection which undeniably exists between all the portions of the dream-thoughts by combining the whole material into a single situation. They reproduce *logical connection* by *approximation in time and space*, just as a painter will represent all the poets in a single group in a picture of Parnassus. It is true that they were never in fact assembled on a single mountain-top; but they certainly form a conceptual group. Dreams carry this method of reproduction down to details; and often when they show us two elements in the dream-content close together, this indicates that there is some specially intimate connection between what correspond to them among the dream-thoughts. Incidentally, it is to be observed that all dreams produced during a single night will be found on analysis to be derived from the same circle of thoughts.

A *causal relation* between two thoughts is either left unrepresented or is replaced by a *sequence* of two pieces of dream of different lengths. Here the representation is often reversed, the beginning of the dream standing for the consequence and its conclusion for the premise. An immediate *transformation* of one thing into another in a dream seems to represent the relation of *cause and effect*.

The alternative '*either–or*' is never expressed in dreams, both of the alternatives being inserted in the text of the dream as though they were equally valid. I have already mentioned that an 'either–or' used in *recording* a dream is to be translated by 'and'.

Ideas which are contraries are by preference expressed in dreams by one and the same element.[10] 'No' seems not to exist so far as dreams are concerned. Opposition between two thoughts, the relation of *reversal*, may be represented in dreams in a most remarkable way. It may be represented by some *other* piece of the dream-content being turned into its opposite – as it were by an after-thought. We shall hear presently of a further method of expressing contradiction. The sensation of *inhibition of movement* which is so common in dreams also serves to express a contradiction between two impulses, a *conflict of will*.

One and one only of these logical relations – that of *similarity, consonance, the possession of common attributes* – is very highly favoured by the mechanism of dream-formation. The dream-work makes use of such cases as a foundation for dream-condensation, by bringing together everything that shows an agreement of this kind into a new unity.

This short series of rough comments is of course inadequate to deal with the full extent of the formal means employed by dreams for the expression of logical relations in the dream-thoughts. Different dreams are more or less carefully constructed in this respect; they keep more or less closely to the text presented to them; they make more or less use of the expedients that are open to the dream-work. In the second case they appear obscure, confused and disconnected. If, however, a dream strikes one as *obviously* absurd, if its content includes a piece of palpable nonsense, this is intentionally so; its apparent disregard of all the requirements of logic is expressing a piece of the intellectual content of the dream-thoughts. Absurdity in a dream signifies the presence in the dream-thoughts of *contradiction, ridicule and derision.* Since this statement is in the most marked opposition to the view that dreams are the product of a dissociated and uncritical mental activity, I will emphasize it by means of an example.

One of my acquaintances, Herr M., had been attacked in an essay with an unjustifiable degree of violence, as we all thought – by no less a person than Goethe. Herr M. was naturally crushed by the attack. He complained of it bitterly to some company at table; his veneration for Goethe had not been affected, however, by this personal experience. I now tried to throw a little light on the chronological data, which seemed to me improbable. Goethe died in 1832. Since his attack on Herr M. must naturally have been made earlier than that, Herr M. must have been quite a young man at the time. It seemed to be a plausible notion that he was eighteen. I was not quite sure, however, what year we were actually in, so that my whole calculation melted into obscurity. Incidentally, the attack was contained in Goethe's well-known essay on 'Nature'.

The nonsensical character of this dream will be even more glaringly obvious, if I explain that Herr M. is a youngish business man, who is far removed from any poetical and literary interests. I have no doubt, however, that when I have entered into the analysis of the dream I shall succeed in showing how much 'method' there is in its nonsense.

The material of the dream was derived from three sources:

(1) Herr M., whom I had got to know among some *company at table*, asked me one day to examine his elder brother, who was showing signs of [general paralysis]. In the course of my conversation with the patient an awkward episode occurred, for he gave his brother away for no accountable reason by talking of his *youthful follies*. I had asked the patient the *year of his birth* (cf. the *year of* Goethe's *death* in the dream) and had made him carry out a number of calculations in order to test the weakness of his memory.

(2) A medical journal, which bore my name among others on its title-page, had published a positively '*crushing*' criticism by a *youthful* reviewer of a book by my friend F.[11] in Berlin. I took the editor to task over this; but, though he expressed his regret, he would not undertake to offer any redress. I therefore severed my connection with the journal, but in my letter of resignation expressed a hope that *our personal relations would not be affected by the event*. This was the true source of the dream. The unfavourable reception of my friend's work had made a profound impression on me. It contained, in my opinion, a fundamental biological discovery, which is only now – many years later – beginning to find favour with the experts.

(3) A woman patient of mine had given me an account a short time before of her brother's illness, and how he had broken out in a frenzy with cries of '*Nature! Nature!*' The doctors believed that his exclamation came from his

having read *Goethe*'s striking essay on that subject and that it showed he had been overworking at his studies. I had remarked that *it seemed to me more plausible* that his exclamation of the word 'Nature' should be taken in the sexual sense in which it is used by the less educated people here. This idea of mine was at least not disproved by the fact that the unfortunate young man subsequently mutilated his own genitals. He was *eighteen* at the time of his outbreak.

Behind my own ego in the dream-content there lay concealed, in the first instance, my friend who had been so badly treated by the critic. '*I tried to throw a little light on the chronological data.*' My friend's book dealt with the *chronological data* of life and among other things showed that the length of *Goethe*'s life was a multiple of a number of days that has a significance in biology. But this ego was compared with a paralytic: '*I was not quite sure what year we were in.*' Thus the dream made out that my friend was behaving like a paralytic, and in this respect it was a mass of absurdities. The dream-thoughts, however, were saying ironically: 'Naturally, it's *he* [my friend F.] who is the crazy fool and it's *you* [the critics] who are the men of genius and know better. Surely it couldn't be the *reverse*?' There were plenty of examples of this *reversal* in the dream. For instance, Goethe attacked the young man, which is absurd, whereas it is still easy for quite a young man to attack the great Goethe.

I should like to lay it down that no dream is prompted by motives other than egoistic ones.[12] In fact, the ego in the

No dream is prompted by motives other than egoistic ones

present dream does not stand only for my friend but for myself as well. I was identifying myself with him, because the fate of his discovery seemed to foreshadow the reception of my own findings. If I were to bring forward my theory emphasizing the part played by sexuality in the aetiology of psychoneurotic disorders (cf. the allusion to the eighteen-year-old patient's cry of 'Nature! Nature!'), I should come across the same criticisms; and I was already preparing to meet them with the same derision.

If we pursue the dream-thoughts further, we shall keep on finding ridicule and derision as correlates of the absurdities of the manifest dream. It is well known that it was the discovery of the split skull of a sheep on the Lido of Venice that gave Goethe the idea of the so-called 'vertebral' theory of the skull. My friend boasts that, when he was a student, he released a storm which led to the resignation of an old professor who, though he had once been distinguished (among other things in connection precisely with the same branch of comparative anatomy), had become incapable of teaching owing to *senile dementia*. Thus the agitation which my friend promoted served to combat the mischievous system according to which there is no *age limit* for academic workers in German universities – for *age is proverbially no defence against folly.* – In the hospital here I had the honour of serving for years under a chief who had long been a *fossil* and had for decades been notoriously *feeble-minded*, but who was allowed to continue carrying on his responsible duties. At this point I thought of a descriptive term based upon the discovery on the lido.[13] Some of my young contemporaries at the hospital concocted, in connection with this man, a version of what was then a popular song: '*Das hat kein Goethe g'schrieben, das hat kein Schiller g'dicht . . .*'[14]

VII

We have not yet come to the end of our consideration of the dream-work. In addition to condensation, displacement and pictorial arrangement of the psychical material, we are obliged to assign it yet another activity, though this is not to be found in operation in *every* dream. I shall not deal exhaustively with this part of the dream-work, and will therefore merely remark that the easiest way of forming an idea of its nature is to suppose – though the supposition probably does not meet the facts – that *it only comes into operation* AFTER *the dream-content has already been constructed*. Its function would then consist in arranging the constituents of the dream in such a way that they form an approximately connected whole, a dream-composition. In this way the dream is given a kind of façade (though this does not, it is true, hide its content at every point), and thus receives a first, preliminary interpretation, which is supported by interpolations and slight modifications. Incidentally, this revision of the dream-content is only possible if it is not too punctiliously carried out; nor does it present us with anything more than a glaring misunderstanding of the dream-thoughts. Before we start upon the analysis of a dream we have to clear the ground of this attempt at an interpretation.

The motive for this part of the dream-work is particularly obvious. *Considerations of intelligibility* are what lead to this final revision of a dream; and this reveals the origin of the activity. It behaves towards the dream-content lying before it just as our normal psychical activity behaves in general towards any perceptual content that may be presented to it. It understands that content on the basis of certain anticipatory ideas, and arranges it, even at the moment of perceiving it, on the presupposition of its being intelligible; in so doing it runs a risk of falsifying it, and in fact, if it cannot bring it into line with anything familiar, is a prey to the strangest misunderstandings. As is well known, we are incapable of seeing a series of unfamiliar signs or of hearing a succession of unknown words, without at once falsifying the perception from considerations of intelligibility, on the basis of something already known to us.

Dreams which have undergone a revision of this kind at the hands of a psychical activity completely analogous to waking thought may be described as 'well-constructed'. In the case of other dreams this activity has completely broken down; no attempt even has been made to arrange or interpret the material, and, since after we have woken up we feel ourselves identical with this last part of the dream-work, we make a judgement that the dream was 'hopelessly confused'. From the point of view of analysis, however, a dream that resembles a disordered heap of disconnected fragments is just as valuable as one that has been beautifully polished and provided with a surface. In the former case, indeed, we are saved the trouble of demolishing what has been superimposed upon the dream-content.

It would be a mistake, however, to suppose that these dream-façades are nothing other than mistaken and somewhat arbitrary revisions of the dream-content by the conscious agency of our mental life. In the erection of a dream-façade use is not infrequently made of wishful phantasies which are present in the dream-thoughts in a pre-constructed form, and are of the same character as the appropriately named 'day-dreams' familiar to us in waking life. The wishful phantasies revealed by analysis in night-dreams often turn out to be repetitions or modified versions of scenes from infancy; thus in some cases the façade of the dream directly reveals the dream's actual nucleus, distorted by an admixture of other material.

The dream-work exhibits no activities other than the four that have already been mentioned. If we keep to the definition of 'dream-work' as the process of transforming the dream-thoughts into the dream-content, it follows that the dream-work is not creative, that it develops no phantasies of its own, that it makes no judgements and draws no conclusions; it has no functions whatever other than condensation and displacement of the material and its modification into pictorial form, to which must be added as a variable factor the final bit of interpretative revision. It is true that we find various things in the dream-content which we should be inclined to regard as a product of some other and higher intellectual function; but in every case analysis shows convincingly that *these intellectual operations have already been performed in the dream-thoughts and have only been* TAKEN OVER *by the dream-content*. A conclusion drawn in a dream is nothing other than the repetition of a conclusion in the dream-thoughts; if the conclusion is taken over into the dream unmodified, it will appear impeccable; if the dream-work has displaced it on to some other material, it will appear nonsensical. A calculation in the dream-content signifies nothing more than that there is a calculation in the dream-thoughts; but while the latter is always rational, a dream-calculation may produce the wildest results if its factors are condensed or if its mathematical operations are displaced on to other material. Not even the speeches that occur in the dream-content are original compositions; they turn out to be a hotchpotch of speeches made, heard or read, which have been revived in the dream-thoughts and whose wording is exactly reproduced, while their origin is entirely disregarded and their meaning is violently changed.

It will perhaps be as well to support these last assertions by a few examples.

(1) Here is an innocent-sounding, well-constructed dream dreamt by a woman patient:

She dreamt she was going to the market with her cook, who was carrying the basket. After she had asked for something, the butcher said to her: 'That's not obtainable any longer,' and offered her something else, adding: 'This is good too.' She rejected it and went on to the woman who sells vegetables, who tried to get her to buy a peculiar vegetable that was tied up in bundles but was of a black colour. She said: 'I don't recognize that: I won't take it.'

The remark '*That's not obtainable any longer*' originated from the treatment itself. A few days earlier I had explained to the patient in those very words that the earliest memories of childhood were '*not obtainable any longer as such*', but were replaced in analysis by 'transferences' and dreams. So *I* was the butcher.

The second speech – '*I don't recognize that*' – occurred in an entirely different connection. On the previous day she had reproved her cook, who incidentally also appeared in the dream, with the words: '*Behave yourself properly! I don't recognize that!*' meaning, no doubt, that she did not understand such behaviour and would not put up with it. As the result of a displacement, it was the more innocent part of this speech which made its way into the content of the dream; but in the dream-thoughts it was only the other part of the speech that played a part. For the dream-work had reduced to complete unintelligibility and extreme innocence an imaginary situation in which *I* was *behaving improperly* to the lady in a particular way. But this situation which the patient was expecting in her imagination was itself only a new edition of something she had once actually experienced.

(II) Here is an apparently quite meaningless dream containing figures. *She was going to pay for something. Her daughter took 3 florins and 65 kreuzers from her (the mother's) purse. The dreamer said to her: 'What are you doing? It only costs 21 kreuzers.'*

The dreamer came from abroad and her daughter was at school here. She was in a position to carry on her treatment with me as long as her daughter remained in Vienna. The day before the dream the headmistress had suggested to her that she should leave her daughter at school for another year. In that case she could also have continued her treatment for a year. The figures in the dream become significant if we remember that 'time is money'. One year is equal to 365 days, or, expressed in money, 365 kreuzers or 3 florins 65 kreuzers. The 21 kreuzers corresponded to the 3 weeks which had still to run between the dream-day and the end of the school term and also to the end of the patient's treatment. It was clearly financial considerations which had induced the lady to refuse the headmistress's proposal, and which were responsible for the smallness of the sums mentioned in the dream.

(III) A lady who, though she was still young, had been married for a number of years, received news that an acquaintance of hers, Fräulein Elise L., who was almost exactly her contemporary, had become engaged. This was the precipitating cause of the following dream:

She was at the theatre with her husband. One side of the stalls was completely empty. Her husband told her that Elise L. and her fiancé had wanted to go too, but had only been able to get bad seats – three for 1 florin 50 kreuzers – and of course they could not take those. She thought it would not really have done any harm if they had.

What interests us here is the source of the figures in the material of the dream-thoughts and the transformations which they underwent. What was the origin of the 1 florin 50 kreuzers? It came from what was in fact an indifferent event of the previous day. Her sister-in-law had been given a present of 150 florins by her husband and had *been in a hurry* to get rid of them by buying a piece of jewellery. It is to be noticed that 150 florins is a *hundred* times as much as 1 florin 50 kreuzers. The only connection with the 'three', which was the number of the theatre tickets, was that her newly engaged friend was that number of months – three – her junior. The situation in the dream was a repetition of a small incident which her husband often teased her about. On one occasion she had been in a great hurry to buy tickets for a play in advance, and when she got to the theatre she had found that one side of the stalls was almost completely empty. There had been *no need for her to be in such a hurry*. Finally, we must not overlook the *absurdity* in the dream of two people taking three tickets for a play.

Now for the dream-thoughts: 'It was *absurd* to marry so early. There was *no need for me to be in such a hurry.* I see from Elise L.'s example that I should have got a husband in the end. Indeed, I should have got one *a hundred times* better' (a treasure) 'if I had only waited. My money' (or dowry) 'could have bought *three* men just as good.'

VIII

Having been made acquainted with the dream-work by the foregoing discussion, we shall no doubt be inclined to pronounce it a quite peculiar psychical process, the like of which, so far as we are aware, does not exist elsewhere. It is as though we were carrying over on to the dream-work all the astonishment which used formerly to be aroused in us by its product, the dream. In fact, however, the dream-work is only the first to be discovered of a whole series of psychical processes, responsible for the generation of hysterical symptoms, of phobias, obsessions and delusions. Condensation and, above all, displacement are invariable characteristics of these other processes as well. Modification into a pictorial form, on the other hand, remains a peculiarity of the dream-work. If this explanation places dreams in a single series alongside the structures produced by psychical illness, this makes it all the more important for us to discover the essential determining conditions of such processes as those of dream-formation. We shall probably be surprised to hear that neither the state of sleep nor illness is among these indispensable conditions. A whole number of the phenomena of the everyday life of healthy people – such as forgetting, slips of the tongue, bungled actions and a particular class of errors – owe their origin to a psychical mechanism analogous to that of dreams and of the other members of the series.

The heart of the problem lies in displacement, which is by far the most striking of the special achievements of the dream-work. If we enter deeply into the subject, we come to realize that the essential determining condition of displacement is a purely psychological one: something in the nature of a *motive*. One comes upon its track if one takes into consideration certain experiences which one cannot escape in analysing dreams. In analysing my specimen dream I was obliged to break off my report of the dream-thoughts on page 12, because, as I confessed, there were some among them which I should prefer to conceal from strangers and which I could not communicate to other people without doing serious mischief in important directions. I added that nothing would be gained if I were to choose another dream instead of that particular one with a view to reporting its analysis: I should come upon dream-thoughts which required to be kept secret in the case of *every* dream with an obscure or confused content. If, however, I were to continue the analysis on my own account, without any reference to other people (whom, indeed, an experience so personal as my dream cannot possibly have been intended to reach), I should eventually arrive at thoughts which would surprise me, whose presence in me I was unaware of, which were not only *alien* but also *disagreeable* to me, and which I should therefore feel inclined to dispute energetically, although the chain of thoughts running through the analysis insisted upon them remorselessly. There is only one way of accounting for this state of affairs, which is of quite universal occurrence; and that is to suppose that these thoughts really were present in my mind, and in possession of a certain amount of psychical intensity or energy, but that they were in a peculiar psychological situation, as a consequence of which they *could not become conscious* to me. (I describe this particular condition as one of 'repression'.) We cannot help concluding, then, that there is a causal connection between the obscurity of the dream-content and the state of repression (inadmissibility to consciousness) of certain of the dream-thoughts, and that the dream had to be obscure so as not to betray the proscribed dream-thoughts. Thus we are led to the concept of a 'dream-distortion', which is the product of the dream-work and serves the purpose of dissimulation, that is, of disguise.

I will test this on the specimen dream which I chose for analysis, and enquire what the thought was which made its way into that dream in a distorted form, and which I should be inclined to repudiate if it were undistorted. I recall that my free cab-drive reminded me of my recent expensive drive with a member of my family, that the interpretation of the dream was 'I wish I might for once experience love that cost me nothing', and that a short time before the dream I had been obliged to spend a considerable sum of money on this same person's account. Bearing this context in mind, I cannot escape the conclusion that *I regret having made that expenditure*. Not until I have recognized this impulse does my wish in the dream for the love which would call for *no* expenditure acquire a meaning. Yet I can honestly say that when I decided to spend this sum of money I did not hesitate for a moment. My regret at having to do so – the contrary current of feeling – did not become conscious to me. *Why* it did not, is another and a far-reaching question, the answer to which is known to me but belongs in another connection.

If the dream that I analyse is not my own, but someone else's, the conclusion will be the same, though the grounds for believing it will be different. If the dreamer is a healthy person, there is no other means open to me of obliging him to recognize the repressed ideas that have been discovered than by pointing out the context of the dream-thoughts; and I cannot help it if he refuses to recognize them. If, however, I am dealing with a neurotic patient, with a hysteric for instance, he will find the acceptance of the repressed thought forced upon him, owing to its connection with the symptoms of his illness, and owing to the improvement he experiences when he exchanges those symptoms for the repressed ideas. In the case, for instance, of the woman patient who had the dream I have just quoted about the three theatre tickets which cost 1 florin 50 kreuzers, the analysis led to the inevitable conclusion that she had a low estimate of her husband (cf. her idea that she could have got one 'a hundred times better'), that she regretted having married him, and that she would have liked to exchange him for another one. It is true that she asserted that she loved her husband, and that her emotional life knew nothing of any such low estimate of him, but all her symptoms led to the same conclusion as the dream. And after her repressed memories had been revived of a particular period during which she had consciously not loved her husband, her symptoms cleared up and her resistance against the interpretation of the dream disappeared.

IX

Now that we have established the concept of repression and have brought dream-distortion into relation with repressed psychical material, we can express in general terms the principal finding to which we have been led by the analysis of dreams. In the case of dreams which are intelligible and have a meaning, we have found that they are undisguised wish-fulfilments; that is, that in their case the dream-situation represents as fulfilled a wish which is known to consciousness, which is left over from daytime life, and which is deservedly of interest. Analysis has taught us something entirely analogous in the case of obscure and confused dreams: once again the dream-situation represents a wish as fulfilled – a wish which invariably arises from the dream-thoughts, but one which is represented in an unrecognizable form and can only be explained when it has been traced back in analysis. The wish in such cases is either itself a repressed one and alien to consciousness, or it is intimately connected with repressed thoughts and is based upon them. Thus the formula for such dreams is as follows: *they are disguised fulfilments of repressed wishes*. It is interesting in this connection to observe that the popular belief that dreams always foretell the future is confirmed. Actually the future which the dream shows us is not the one which *will* occur but the one which we should *like* to occur. The popular mind is behaving here as it usually does: what it wishes, it believes.

Dreams fall into three classes according to their attitude to wish-fulfilment. The first class consists of those which represent an unrepressed wish undisguisedly; these are the dreams of an infantile type which become ever rarer in adults. Secondly there are the dreams which express a repressed wish disguisedly; these no doubt form the overwhelming majority of all our dreams, and require analysis before they can be understood. In the third place there are the dreams which represent a repressed wish, but do so with insufficient or no disguise. These last dreams are invariably accompanied by anxiety, which interrupts them. In their case anxiety takes the place of dream-distortion; and in dreams of the second class anxiety is only avoided owing to the dream-work. There is no great difficulty in proving that the ideational content which produces anxiety in us in dreams was once a wish but has since undergone repression.

There are also clear dreams with a distressing content, which, however, is not felt as distressing in the dream itself. For this reason they cannot be counted as anxiety-dreams; but they have always been taken as evidence of the fact that dreams are without meaning and have no psychical value. An analysis of a dream of this kind will show that we are dealing with well-disguised fulfilments of repressed wishes, that is to say with a dream of the second class; it will also show how admirably the process of displacement is adapted for disguising wishes.

A girl had a dream of seeing her sister's only surviving child lying dead in the same surroundings in which a few years earlier she had in fact seen the dead body of her sister's *first* child. She felt no pain over this; but she naturally rejected the idea that this situation represented any wish of hers. Nor was there any need to suppose this. It had been beside the first child's coffin, however, that, years before, she had seen and spoken to the man she was in love with; if the second child died, she would no doubt meet the man again in her sister's house. She longed for such a meeting, but fought against the feeling. On the dream-day she had bought a ticket for a lecture which was to be given by this same man, to whom she was still devoted. Her dream was a simple dream of impatience of the kind that often occurs before journeys, visits to the theatre, and similar enjoyments that lie ahead. But in order to disguise this longing from her, the situation was displaced on to an event of a kind most unsuitable for producing a feeling of enjoyment, though it had in fact done so in the past. It is to be observed that the emotional behaviour in the dream was appropriate to the real content which lay in the background and not to what was pushed into the foreground. The dream-situation anticipated the meeting she had so long desire; it offered no basis for any painful feelings.

X

Hitherto philosophers have had no occasion to concern themselves with a psychology of repression. We may therefore be permitted to make a first approach to this hitherto unknown topic by constructing a pictorial image of the course of events in dream-formation. It is true that the schematic picture we have arrived at – not only from the study of dreams – is a fairly complicated one; but we cannot manage with anything simpler. Our hypothesis is that in our mental apparatus there are two thought-constructing agencies, of which the second enjoys the privilege of having free access to consciousness for its products, whereas the activity of the first is in itself unconscious and can only reach consciousness by way of the second. On the frontier between the two agencies, where the first passes over to the second, there is a censorship, which only allows what is agreeable to it to pass through and holds back everything else. According to our definition, then, what is rejected by the censorship is in a state of repression. Under certain conditions, of which the state of sleep is one, the relation between the strength of the two agencies is modified in such a way that what is repressed can no longer be held back. In the state of sleep this probably occurs owing to a relaxation of the censorship; when this happens it becomes possible for what has hitherto been repressed to make a path for itself to consciousness. Since, however, the censorship is never completely eliminated but merely reduced, the repressed material must submit to certain alterations which mitigate its offensive features. What becomes conscious in such cases is a compromise between the intentions of one agency and the demands of the other. *Repression – relaxation of the censorship – the formation of a compromise*, this is the fundamental pattern for the generation not only of dreams but of many other psychopathological structures; and in the latter cases too we may observe that the formation of compromises is accompanied by processes of condensation and displacement and by the employment of superficial associations, which we have become familiar with in the dream-work.

We have no reason to disguise the fact that in the hypothesis which we have set up in order to explain the dream-work a part is played by what might be described as a 'daemonic' element. We have gathered an impression that the formation of obscure dreams occurs *as though* one person who was dependent upon a second person had to make a remark which was bound to be disagreeable in the ears of this second one; and it is on the basis of this simile that we have arrived at the concepts of dream-distortion and censorship, and have endeavoured to translate our impression into a psychological theory which is no doubt crude but is at least lucid. Whatever it may be with which a further investigation of the subject may enable us to identify our first and second agencies, we may safely expect to find a confirmation of some correlate of our hypothesis that the second agency controls access to consciousness and can bar the first agency from such access.

When the state of sleep is over, the censorship quickly recovers its full strength; and it can now wipe out all that was won from it during the period of its weakness. This must be one part at least of the explanation of the forgetting of dreams, as is shown by an observation which has been confirmed on countless occasions. It not infrequently happens that during the narration of a dream or during its analysis a fragment of the dream-content which had seemed to be forgotten re-emerges. This fragment which has been rescued from oblivion invariably affords us the best and most direct access to the meaning of the dream. And that, in all probability, must have been the only reason for its having been forgotten, that is, for its having been once more suppressed.

XI

When once we have recognized that the content of a dream is the representation of a fulfilled wish and that its obscurity is due to alterations in repressed material made by the censorship, we shall no longer have any difficulty in discovering the *function* of dreams. It is commonly said that sleep is disturbed by dreams; strangely enough, we are led to a contrary view and must regard dreams as *the guardians of sleep*.

In the case of children's dreams there should be no difficulty in accepting this statement. The state of sleep or the psychical modification involved in sleep, whatever that may be, is brought about by a resolve to sleep which is either imposed upon the child or is reached on the basis of sensations of fatigue; and it is only made possible by the withholding of stimuli which might suggest to the psychical apparatus aims other than that of sleeping. The means by which *external* stimuli can be kept off are familiar to us; but what are the means available for controlling *internal* mental stimuli which set themselves against falling asleep?

Let us observe a mother putting her child to sleep. The child gives vent to an unceasing stream of desires: he wants one more kiss, he wants to go on playing. His mother satisfies some of these desires, but uses her authority to postpone others of them to the next day. It is clear that any wishes or needs that may arise have an inhibiting effect upon falling asleep. We all know the amusing story told by Balduin Groller [a popular nineteenth-century Austrian novelist] of the bad little boy who woke up in the middle of the night and shouted across the night-nursery: 'I want the rhino!' A better behaved child, instead of shouting, would have *dreamt* that he was playing with the rhino. Since a dream that shows a wish as fulfilled is *believed* during sleep, it does away with the wish and makes sleep possible. It cannot be disputed that dream-images are believed in in this way, for they are clothed in the psychical appearance of perceptions, and children have not yet acquired the later faculty of distinguishing hallucinations or phantasies from reality.

Adults have learnt to make this distinction; they have also grasped the uselessness of wishing, and after lengthy practice know how to postpone their desires until they can find satisfaction by the long and roundabout path of altering the external world. In their case, accordingly, wish-fulfilments along the short psychical path are rare in sleep too; it is even possible, indeed, that they never occur at all, and that anything that may seem to us to be con- structed on the pattern of a child's dream in fact requires a far more complicated solution. On the other hand, in the case of adults – and this no doubt applies without exception to everyone in full possession of his senses – a differentiation has occurred in the psychical material, which was not present in children. A psychical agency has come into being, which, taught by experience of life, exercises a dominating and inhibiting influence upon mental impulses and maintains that influence with jealous severity, and which, owing to its relation to consciousness and to voluntary movement, is armed with the strongest instruments of psychical power. A portion of the impulses of childhood has been suppressed by this agency as being useless to life, and any thought-material derived from those impulses is in a state of repression.

Now while this agency, in which we recognize our normal ego, is concentrated on the wish to sleep, it appears to be compelled by the psycho-physiological conditions of sleep to relax the energy with which it is accustomed to hold down the repressed material during the day. In itself, no doubt, this relaxation does no harm; however much the suppressed impulses of the childish mind may prance around, their access to consciousness is still difficult and their access to movement is barred, as the result of this same state of sleep. The danger of sleep being disturbed by them must, however, be guarded against. We must in any case suppose that even during deep sleep a certain amount of free attention is on duty as a guard against sensory stimuli, and that this guard may sometimes consider waking more advisable than a continuation of sleep. Otherwise there would be no explanation of how it is that we can be woken up at any moment by sensory stimuli of some particular *quality*. As the physiologist Burdach [1838, 486] insisted long ago, a mother, for instance, will be roused by the whimpering of her baby, or a miller if his mill comes to a stop, or most people if they are called softly by their own name. Now the attention which is thus on guard is also directed towards internal wishful stimuli arising from the repressed material, and combines with them to form the dream which, as a compromise, simultaneously satisfies both of the two agencies. The dream provides a kind of psychical consummation for the wish that has been suppressed (or formed with the help of repressed material) by representing it as fulfilled; but it also satisfies the other agency by allowing sleep to continue. In this respect our ego is ready to behave like a child; it gives credence to the dream-images, as though what it wanted to say was: 'Yes, yes! you're quite right, but let me go on sleeping!' The low estimate which we form of dreams when we are awake, and which we relate to their confused and apparently illogical character, is probably nothing other than the judgement passed by our sleeping ego upon the repressed impulses, a judgement based, with better right, upon the motor impotence of these disturbers of sleep. We are sometimes aware in our sleep of this contemptuous judgement. If the content of a dream goes too far in overstepping the censorship, we think: 'After all, it's only a dream!' – and go on sleeping.

This view is not traversed by the fact that there are marginal cases in which the dream – as happens with anxiety-dreams – can no longer perform its function of preventing an interruption of sleep, but assumes instead the other function of promptly bringing sleep to an end. In doing so it is merely behaving like a conscientious night-watchman, who first carries out his duty by suppressing disturbances so that the townsmen may not be woken up, but afterwards continues to do his duty by himself waking the townsmen up, if the causes of the disturbance seem to him serious and of a kind that he cannot cope with alone.

The function of the dream as a guardian of sleep becomes particularly evident when an external stimulus impinges upon the senses of a sleeper. It is generally recognized that sensory stimuli arising during sleep influence the content of dreams; this can be proved experimentally and is among the few certain (but, incidentally, greatly overvalued) findings of medical investigation into dreams. But this finding involves a puzzle which has hitherto proved insoluble. For the sensory stimulus which the experimenter causes to impinge upon the sleeper is not correctly recognized in the dream; it is subjected to one of an indefinite number of possible interpretations, the choice being apparently left to an arbitrary psychical determination. But there is, of course, no such thing as arbitrary determination in the mind. There are several ways in which a sleeper may react to an external sensory stimulus. He may wake up or he may succeed in continuing his sleep in spite of it. In the latter case he may make use of a dream in order to get rid of the external stimulus, and here again there is more than one method open to him. For instance, he may get rid of the stimulus by dreaming that he is in a situation which is absolutely incompatible with the stimulus. Such was the line taken by a sleeper who was subject to disturbance by a painful abscess on the perineum. He dreamt that he was riding on a horse, making use of the poultice that was intended to mitigate his pain as a saddle, and in this way he avoided being disturbed. Or, as happens more frequently, the external stimulus is given an interpretation which brings it into the context of a repressed wish which is at the moment awaiting fulfilment; in this way the external stimulus is robbed of its reality and is treated as though it were a portion of the psychical material. Thus someone dreamt that he had written a comedy with a particular plot; it was produced in a theatre, the first act was over, and there were thunders of applause; the clapping was terrific . . . The dreamer must have succeeded in prolonging his sleep till after the interference had ceased; for when he woke up he no longer heard the noise, but rightly concluded that someone must have been beating a carpet or mattress. Every dream which occurs immediately before the sleeper is woken by a loud noise had made an attempt at explaining away the arousing stimulus by providing another explanation of it and has thus sought to prolong sleep, even if only for a moment.

XII

No one who accepts the view that the censorship is the chief reason for dream-distortion will be surprised to learn from the results of dream-interpretation that most of the dreams of adults are traced back by analysis to *erotic wishes*. This assertion is not aimed at dreams with an *undisguised* sexual content, which are no doubt familiar to all dreamers from their own experience and are as a rule the only ones to be described as 'sexual dreams'. Even dreams of this latter kind offer enough surprises in their choice of the people whom they make into sexual objects, in their disregard of all the limitations which the dreamer imposes in his waking life upon his sexual desires, and by their many strange details, hinting at what are commonly known as 'perversions'. A great many other dreams, however, which show no sign of being erotic in their manifest content, are revealed by the work of interpretation in analysis as sexual wish-fulfilments; and, on the other hand, analysis proves that a great many of the thoughts left over from the activity of waking life as 'residues of the previous day' only find their way to representation in dreams through the assistance of repressed erotic wishes.

There is no theoretical necessity why this should be so; but to explain the fact it may be pointed out that no other group of instincts has been submitted to such far-reaching suppression by the demands of cultural education, while at the same time the sexual instincts are also the ones which, in most people, find it easiest to escape from the control of the highest mental agencies. Since we have become acquainted with infantile sexuality, which is often so unobtrusive in its manifestations and is always overlooked and misunderstood, we are justified in saying that almost every civilized man retains the infantile forms of sexual life in some respect or other. We can thus understand how it is that repressed infantile sexual wishes provide the most frequent and strongest motive-forces for the construction of dreams.[15]

There is only one method by which a dream which expresses erotic wishes can succeed in appearing innocently non-sexual in its manifest content. The material of the sexual ideas must not be represented as such, but must be replaced in the content of the dream by hints, allusions and similar forms of indirect representation. But, unlike other forms of indirect representation, that which is employed in dreams must not be immediately intelligible. The modes of representation which fulfil these conditions are usually described as 'symbols' of the things which they represent. Particular interest has been directed to them since it has been noticed that dreamers speaking the same language make use of the same

symbols, and that in some cases, indeed, the use of the
same symbols extends beyond the use of the same language. Since dreamers themselves are unaware of the
meaning of the symbols they use, it is difficult at first
sight to discover the source of the connection between
the symbols and what they replace and represent. The fact
itself, however, is beyond doubt, and it is important for
the technique of dream-interpretation. For, with the help
of a knowledge of dream-symbolism, it is possible to
understand the meaning of separate elements of the content of a dream or separate pieces of a dream or in some
cases even whole dreams, without having to ask the
dreamer for his associations.[16] Here we are approaching
the popular ideal of translating dreams and on the other
hand are returning to the technique of interpretation
used by the ancients, to whom dream-interpretation was
identical with interpretation by means of symbols.

Although the study of dream-symbols is far from being
complete, we are in a position to lay down with certainty
a number of general statements and a quantity of special
information on the subject. There are some symbols
which bear a single meaning almost universally: thus the
Emperor and Empress (or the King and Queen) stand for
the parents, rooms represent women[17] and their entrances
and exits the openings of the body. The majority of
dream-symbols serve to represent persons, parts of the
body and activities invested with erotic interest; in particular, the genitals are represented by a number of often

very surprising symbols, and the greatest variety of objects are employed to denote them symbolically. Sharp weapons, long and stiff objects, such as tree-trunks and sticks, stand for the male genital; while cupboards, boxes, carriages or ovens may represent the uterus. In such cases as these the *tertium comparationis*, the common element in these substitutions, is immediately intelligible; but there are other symbols in which it is not so easy to grasp the connection. Symbols such as a staircase or going upstairs to represent sexual intercourse, a tie or cravat for the male organ, or wood for the female one, provoke our unbelief until we can arrive at an understanding of the symbolic relation underlying them by some other means. Moreover a whole number of dream-symbols are bisexual and can relate to the male or female genitals according to the context.

Some symbols are universally disseminated and can be met with in all dreamers belonging to a single linguistic or cultural group; there are others which occur only within the most restricted and individual limits, symbols constructed by an individual out of his own ideational material. Of the former class we can distinguish some whose claim to represent sexual ideas is immediately justified by linguistic usage (such, for instance, as those derived from agriculture, e.g. 'fertilization' or 'seed') and others whose relation to sexual ideas appears to reach back into the very earliest ages and to the most obscure depths of our conceptual functioning. The power of constructing symbols has not been exhausted in our own days in the case of either of the two sorts of symbols which I have distinguished at the beginning of this paragraph. Newly discovered objects (such as airships) are, as we may observe, at once adopted as universally available sexual symbols.

It would, incidentally, be a mistake to expect that if we had a still profounder knowledge of dream-symbolism (of the 'language of dreams') we could do without asking the dreamer for his associations to the dream and go back entirely to the technique of dream-interpretation of antiquity. Quite apart from individual symbols and oscillations in the use of universal ones, one can never tell whether any particular element in the content of a dream is to be interpreted symbolically or in its proper sense, and one can be certain that the *whole* content of a dream is not to be interpreted symbolically. A knowledge of dream-symbolism will never do more than enable us to translate certain constituents of the dream-content, and will not relieve us of the necessity for applying the technical rules which I gave earlier. It will, however, afford the most valuable assistance to interpretation precisely at points at which the dreamer's associations are insufficient or fail altogether.

Dream-symbolism is also indispensable to an understanding of what are known as 'typical' dreams, which are common to everyone, and of 'recurrent' dreams in individuals.

If the account I have given in this short discussion of the symbolic mode of expression in dreams appears incomplete, I can justify my neglect by drawing attention to one of the most important pieces of knowledge that we possess on this subject. Dream-symbolism extends far beyond dreams: it is not peculiar to dreams, but exercises a similar dominating influence on representation in fairytales, myths and legends, in jokes and in folk-lore. It enables us to trace the intimate connections between dreams and these latter productions. We must not suppose that dream-symbolism is a creation of the dream-work; it is in all probability a characteristic of the unconscious thinking which provides the dream-work with the material for condensation, displacement and dramatization.[18]

XIII

I lay no claim to have thrown light in these pages upon *all* the problems of dreams, nor to having dealt in a convincing way with those that I *have* discussed. Anyone who is interested in the whole extent of the literature of dreams may be referred to a work by Sante de Sanctis (*I sogni*, 1899); and anyone who wishes to hear more detailed arguments in favour of the view of dreams which I myself have put forward should turn to my volume *The Interpretation of Dreams*, 1900. It only remains for me now to indicate the direction in which my exposition of the subject of the dream-work calls for pursuit.

I have laid it down as the task of dream-interpretation to replace the dream by the latent dream-thoughts, that is, to unravel what the dream-work has woven. In so doing I have raised a number of new psychological problems dealing with the mechanism of this dream-work itself, as well as with the nature and conditions of what is described as repression; on the other hand I have asserted the existence of the dream-thoughts – a copious store of psychical structures of the highest order, which is characterized by all the signs of normal intellectual functioning, but is nevertheless withdrawn from consciousness till it emerges in distorted form in the dream-content. I cannot but assume that thoughts of this kind are present in everyone, since almost everyone, including the most normal people, is capable of dreaming. The unconscious material of the dream-thoughts and its relation to consciousness and to repression raise further questions of significance to psychology, the answers to which must no doubt be postponed until analysis has clarified the origin of other psychopathological structures, such as hysterical symptoms and obsessional ideas.

Typical Dreams, from *The Interpretation of Dreams*

WE ARE NOT in general in a position to interpret another person's dream unless he is prepared to communicate to us the unconscious thoughts that lie behind its content. The practical applicability of our method of interpreting dreams is in consequence severely restricted.[1] We have seen that, as a general rule, each person is at liberty to construct his dream-world according to his individual peculiarities and so to make it unintelligible to other people. It now appears, however, that, in complete contrast to this, there are a certain number of dreams which almost everyone has dreamt alike and which we are accustomed to assume must have the same meaning for everyone. A special interest attaches, moreover, to these typical dreams because they presumably arise from the same sources in every case and thus seem particularly well qualified to throw light on the sources of dreams.

It is therefore with quite particular anticipations that we shall attempt to apply our technique of dream-interpretation to these typical dreams; and it is with great reluctance that we shall have to confess that our art disappoints our expectations precisely in relation to this material. If we attempt to interpret a typical dream, the dreamer fails as a rule to produce the associations which would in other cases have led us to understand it, or else his associations become obscure and insufficient so that we cannot solve our problem with their help. We shall learn in a later portion of this work[2] why this is so and how we can make up for this defect in our technique. My readers will also discover why it is that at the present point I am able to deal only with a few members of the group of typical dreams and must postpone my consideration of the rest until this later point in my discussion.[3]

(α) Embarrassing Dreams Of Being Naked

Dreams of being naked or insufficiently dressed in the presence of strangers sometimes occur with the additional feature of there being a complete absence of any such feeling as shame on the dreamer's part. We are only concerned here, however, with those dreams of being naked in which one *does* feel shame and embarrassment and tries to escape or hide, and is then overcome by a strange inhibition which prevents one from moving and makes one feel incapable of altering one's distressing situation. It is only with this accompaniment that the dream is typical; without it, the gist of its subject-matter may be included in every variety of context or may be ornamented with individual trimmings. Its essence [in its typical form] lies in a distressing feeling in the nature of shame and in the fact that one wishes to hide one's nakedness, as a rule by locomotion, but finds one is unable to do so. I believe the great majority of my readers will have found themselves in this situation in dreams.

The nature of the undress involved is customarily far from clear. The dreamer may say 'I was in my chemise', but this is rarely a distinct picture. The kind of undress is usually so vague that the description is expressed as an alternative: 'I was in my chemise or petticoat.' As a rule the defect in the dreamer's toilet is not so grave as to appear to justify the shame to which it gives rise. In the case of a man who has worn the Emperor's uniform, nakedness is often replaced by some breach of the dress regulations: 'I was walking in the street without my sabre and saw some officers coming up', or 'I was without my necktie', or 'I was wearing civilian check trousers', and so on.

The people in whose presence one feels ashamed are almost always strangers, with their features left indeterminate. In the typical dream it never happens that the clothing which causes one so much embarrassment is objected to or so much as noticed by the onlookers. On the contrary, they adopt indifferent or (as I observed in one particularly clear dream) solemn and stiff expressions of face. This is a suggestive point.

The embarrassment of the dreamer and the indifference of the onlookers offer us, when taken together, a contradiction of the kind that is so common in dreams. It would after all be more in keeping with the dreamer's feelings if strangers looked at him in astonishment and derision or with indignation. But this objectionable feature of the situation has, I believe, been got rid of by wish-fulfilment, whereas some force has led to the retention of the other features; and the two portions of the dream are consequently out of harmony with each other. We possess an interesting piece of evidence that the dream in the form in which it appears – partly distorted by wish-fulfilment – has not been rightly understood. For it has become the basis of a fairy tale which is familiar to us all in Hans Andersen's version, *The Emperor's New Clothes*, and which has quite recently been put into verse by Ludwig Fulda[4] in his ['dramatic fairy tale'] *Der Talisman*. Hans Andersen's fairy tale tells us how two impostors weave the Emperor a costly garment which, they say, will be visible only to persons of virtue and loyalty. The Emperor walks out in this invisible garment, and all the spectators, intimidated by the fabric's power to act as a touchstone, pretend not to notice the Emperor's nakedness.

This is just the situation in our dream. It is hardly rash to assume that the unintelligibility of the dream's content as it exists in the memory has led to its being recast in a form designed to make sense of the situation. That situation, however, is in the process deprived of its original meaning and put to extraneous uses. But, as we shall see later, it is a common thing for the conscious thought-activity of a second psychical system to misunderstand the content of a dream in this way, and this misunderstanding must be regarded as one of the factors in determining the final form assumed by dreams. Moreover we shall learn that similar misunderstandings (taking place, once again, within one and the same psychical personality) play a major part in the construction of obsessions and phobias.

In the case of our dream we are in a position to indicate the material upon which the misinterpretation is based. The impostor is the dream and the Emperor is the dreamer himself; the moralizing purpose of the dream reveals an obscure knowledge of the fact that the latent dream-content is concerned with forbidden wishes that have fallen victim to repression. For the context in which dreams of this sort appear during my analyses of neurotics leaves no doubt that they are based upon memories from earliest childhood. It is only in our childhood that we are seen in inadequate clothing both by members of our family and by strangers – nurses, maid-servants, and visitors; and it is only then that we feel no shame at our nakedness.[5] We can observe how undressing has an almost intoxicating effect on many children even in their later years, instead of making them feel ashamed. They laugh and jump about and slap themselves, while their mother, or whoever else may be there, reproves them and says: 'Ugh! Shocking! You mustn't ever do that!' Children frequently manifest a desire to exhibit. One can scarcely pass through a country village in our part of the world without meeting some child of two or three who lifts up his little shirt in front of one – in one's honour, perhaps. One of my patients has a conscious memory of a scene in his eighth year, when at bed-time he wanted to dance into the next room where his little sister slept, dressed in his night-shirt, but was prevented by his nurse. In the early history of neurotics an important part is played by exposure to children of the opposite sex; in paranoia delusions of being observed while dressing and undressing are to be traced back to experiences of this kind; while among persons who have remained at the stage of perversion there is one class in which this infantile impulse has reached the pitch of a symptom – the class of 'exhibitionists'.

When we look back at this unashamed period of childhood it seems to us a Paradise; and Paradise itself is no more than a group phantasy of the childhood of the individual. That is why mankind were naked in Paradise and were without shame in one another's presence; till a moment arrived when shame and anxiety awoke, expulsion followed, and sexual life and the tasks of cultural activity began. But we can regain this Paradise every night in our dreams. I have already expressed a suspicion that impressions of earliest childhood (that is, from the prehistoric epoch until about the end of the third year of life) strive to achieve reproduction[6] from their very nature and irrespectively perhaps of their actual content, and that their repetition constitutes the fulfilment of a wish. Thus dreams of being naked are dreams of exhibiting.[7]

The core of a dream of exhibiting lies in the figure of the dreamer himself (not as he was as a child but as he appears at the present time) and his inadequate clothing (which emerges indistinctly, whether owing to superimposed layers of innumerable later memories of being in undress or as a result of the censorship). Added to these are the figures of the people in whose presence the dreamer feels ashamed. I know of no instance in which the actual spectators of the infantile scene of exhibiting have appeared in the dream; a dream is scarcely ever a simple memory. Curiously enough, the people upon whom our sexual interest was directed in childhood are omitted in all the reproductions which occur in dreams, in hysteria and in obsessional neurosis. It is only in paranoia that these spectators reappear and, though they remain invisible, their presence is inferred with fanatical conviction. What takes their place in dreams – 'a lot of strangers' who take no notice of the spectacle that is offered – is nothing more nor less than the wishful contrary of the single familiar individual before whom the dreamer exposed himself. Incidentally, 'a lot of strangers' frequently appear in dreams in many other connections, and they always stand as the wishful contrary of 'secrecy'. It is to be noticed that even in paranoia, where the original state of things is restored, this reversal into a contrary is observed. The subject feels that he is no longer alone, he has no doubt that he is being observed, but the observers are 'a lot of strangers' whose identity is left curiously vague.

In addition to this, repression plays a part in dreams of exhibiting; for the distress felt in such dreams is a reaction on the part of the second system against the content of the scene of exhibiting having found expression in spite of the ban upon it. If the distress was to be avoided, the scene should never have been revived.

We shall return later to the feeling of being inhibited.[8] It serves admirably in dreams to represent a conflict in the will or a negative. The unconscious purpose requires the exhibiting to proceed; the censorship demands that it shall be stopped.

There can be no doubt that the connections between our typical dreams and fairy tales and the material of other kinds of creative writing are neither few nor accidental. It sometimes happens that the sharp eye of a creative writer has an analytic realization of the process of transformation of which he is habitually no more than the tool. If so, he may follow the process in a reverse direction and so trace back the imaginative writing to a dream. One of my friends has drawn my attention to the following passage in Gottfried Keller's *Der grüne Heinrich* [Part III, Chapter 2]: 'I hope, my dear Lee, that you may never learn from your own personal experience the peculiar and *piquant* truth of the plight of Odysseus when he appeared, naked and covered with mud, before the eyes of Nausicaä and her maidens! Shall I tell you how that can happen? Let us look into our example. If you are wandering about in a foreign land, far from your home and from all that you hold dear, if you have seen and heard many things, have known sorrow and care, and are wretched and forlorn, then without fail you will dream one night that you are coming near to your home; you will see it gleaming and shining in the fairest colours, and the sweetest, dearest and most beloved forms will move towards you. Then suddenly you will become aware that you are in rags, naked and dusty. You will be seized with a nameless shame and dread, you will seek to find covering and to hide yourself, and you will awake bathed in sweat. This, so long as men breathe, is the dream of the unhappy wanderer; and Homer has evoked the picture of his plight from the deepest and eternal nature of man.'

The deepest and eternal nature of man, upon whose evocation in his hearers the poet is accustomed to rely, lies in those impulses of the mind which have their roots in a childhood that has since become prehistoric. Suppressed and forbidden wishes from childhood break through in the dream behind the exile's unobjectionable wishes which are capable of entering consciousness;

and that is why the dream which finds concrete expression in the legend of Nausicaä ends as a rule as an anxiety-dream.

My own dream[9] of running upstairs and of soon afterwards finding myself glued to the steps was equally a dream of exhibiting, since it bears the essential marks of being one. It should be possible, therefore, to trace it back to experiences during my childhood, and if these could be discovered they should enable us to judge how far the maid-servant's behaviour to me – her accusing me of dirtying the carpet – helped to give her her place in my dream. I can, as it happens, provide the necessary particulars. In a psychoanalysis one learns to interpret propinquity in time as representing connection in subject-matter.[10] Two thoughts which occur in immediate sequence without any apparent connection are in fact part of a single unity which has to be discovered; in just the same way, if I write an 'a' and a 'b' in succession, they have to be pronounced as a single syllable 'ab'. The same is true of dreams. The staircase dream to which I have referred was one of a series of dreams; and I understood the interpretation of the other members of the series. Since this particular dream was surrounded by the others it must have dealt with the same subject. Now these other dreams were based on a recollection of a nurse in whose charge I had been from some date during my earliest infancy till I was two and a half. I even retain an obscure conscious memory of her. According to what I was told not long ago by my mother, she was old and ugly, but very sharp and efficient. From what I can infer from my own dreams her treatment of me was not always excessive in its amiability and her words could be harsh if I failed to reach the required standard of cleanliness. And thus the maid-servant, since she had undertaken the job of carrying on this educational work, acquired the right to be treated in my dream as a reincarnation of the prehistoric old nurse. It is reasonable to suppose that the child loved the old woman who taught him these lessons, in spite of her rough treatment of him.[11]

(β) Dreams Of The Death Of Persons Of Whom The Dreamer Is Fond

Another group of dreams which may be described as typical are those containing the death of some loved relative – for instance, of a parent, of a brother or sister, or of a child. Two classes of such dreams must at once be distinguished: those in which the dreamer is unaffected by grief, so that on awakening he is astonished at his lack of feeling, and those in which the dreamer feels deeply pained by the death and may even weep bitterly in his sleep.

We need not consider the dreams of the first of these classes, for they have no claim to be regarded as 'typical'. If we analyse them, we find that they have some meaning other than their apparent one, and that they are intended to conceal some other wish. Such was the dream of the aunt who saw her sister's only son lying in his coffin.[12] It did not mean that she wished her little nephew dead; as we have seen, it merely concealed a wish to see a particular person of whom she was fond and whom she had not met for a long time – a person whom she had once before met after a similarly long interval beside the coffin of another nephew. This wish, which was the true content of the dream, gave no occasion for grief, and no grief, therefore, was felt in the dream. It will be noticed that the affect felt in the dream belongs to its latent and not to its manifest content, and that the dream's *affective* content has remained untouched by the distortion which has overtaken its *ideational* content.

Very different are the dreams of the other class – those in which the dreamer imagines the death of a loved relative and is at the same time painfully affected. The meaning of such dreams, as their content indicates, is a wish that the person in question may die. And since I must expect that the feelings of all of my readers and any others who have experienced similar dreams will rebel against my assertion, I must try to base my evidence for it on the broadest possible foundation.

I have already discussed a dream which taught us that the wishes which are represented in dreams as fulfilled are not always present-day wishes. They may also be wishes of the past which have been abandoned, overlaid and repressed, and to which we have to attribute some sort of continued existence only because of their re-emergence in a dream. They are not dead in our sense of the word but only like the shades in the *Odyssey*, which awoke to some sort of life as soon as they had tasted blood. In the dream of the dead child in the 'case'[13] what was involved was a wish which had been an immediate one fifteen years earlier and was frankly admitted as having existed at that time. I may add – and this may not be without its bearing upon the theory of dreams – that even behind this wish there lay a memory from the dreamer's earliest childhood. When she was a small child – the exact date could not be fixed with certainty – she had heard that her mother had fallen into a deep depression during the pregnancy of which she had been the fruit and had passionately wished that the child she was bearing might die. When the dreamer herself was grown-up and pregnant, she merely followed her mother's example.

If anyone dreams, with every sign of pain, that his father or mother or brother or sister has died, I should never use the dream as evidence that he wishes for that person's death *at the present time*. The theory of dreams does not require as much as that; it is satisfied with the inference that this death has been wished for at some time or other during the dreamer's childhood. I fear, however, that this reservation will not appease the objectors; they will deny the possibility of their *ever* having had such a thought with just as much energy as they insist that they harbour no such wishes now. I must therefore reconstruct a portion of the vanished mental life of children on the basis of the evidence of the present.[14]

LET US FIRST consider the relation of children to their brothers and sisters. I do not know why we presuppose that that relation must be a loving one; for instances of hostility between adult brothers and sisters force themselves upon everyone's experience and we can often establish the fact that the disunity originated in childhood or has always existed. But it is further true that a great many adults, who are on affectionate terms with their brothers and sisters and are ready to stand by them to-day, passed their childhood on almost unbroken terms of enmity with them. The elder child ill-treats the younger, maligns him and robs him of his toys; while the younger is consumed with impotent rage against the elder, envies and fears him, or meets his oppressor with the first stirrings of a love of liberty and a sense of justice. Their parents complain that the children do not get on with one another, but cannot discover why. It is easy to see that the character of even a good child is not what we should wish to find it in an adult. Children are completely egoistic; they feel their needs intensely and strive ruthlessly to satisfy them – especially as against the rivals, other children, and first and foremost as against their brothers and sisters. But we do not on that account call a child 'bad', we call him 'naughty'; he is no more answerable for his evil deeds in our judgement than in the eyes of the law. And it is right that this should be so; for we may expect that, before the end of the period which we count as childhood, altruistic impulses and morality will awaken in the little egoist and (to use Meynert's terms [e.g. 1892, 169 ff.]) a secondary ego will overlay and inhibit the primary one. It is true, no doubt, that morality does not set in simultaneously all along the line and that the length of non-moral childhood varies in different individuals. If this morality fails to develop, we like to talk of 'degeneracy', though what in fact faces us is an inhibition in development. After the primary character has already been overlaid by later development, it can still be laid bare again, at all events in part, in cases of hysterical illness. There is a really striking resemblance between what is known as the hysterical character and that of a naughty child. Obsessional neurosis, on the contrary, corresponds to a super-morality imposed as a reinforcing weight upon fresh stirrings of the primary character.

Many people, therefore, who love their brothers and sisters and would feel bereaved if they were to die, harbour evil wishes against them in their unconscious, dating from earlier times; and these are capable of being realized in dreams.

It is of quite particular interest, however, to observe the behaviour of small children up to the age of two or three or a little older towards their younger brothers and sisters. Here, for instance, was a child who had so far been the only one; and now he was told that the stork had brought a new baby. He looked the new arrival up and down and then declared decisively: 'The stork can take him away again!'[15] I am quite seriously of the opinion that a child can form a just estimate of the set-back he has to expect at the hands of the little stranger. A lady of my acquaintance, who is on very good terms to-day with a sister four years her junior, tells me that she greeted the news of her first arrival with this qualification: 'But all the same I shan't give her my red cap.' Even if a child only comes to realize the situation later on, his hostility will date from that moment. I know of a case in which a little girl of less than three tried to strangle an infant in its cradle because she felt that its continued presence boded her no good. Children at that time of life are capable of jealousy of any degree of intensity and obviousness. Again, if it should happen that the baby sister does in fact disappear after a short while, the elder child will find the whole affection of the household once more concentrated upon himself. If after that the stork should bring yet another baby, it seems only logical that the little favourite should nourish a wish that his new competitor may meet with the same fate as the earlier one, so that he himself may be as happy as he was originally and during the interval.[16] Normally, of course, this attitude of a child towards a younger brother or sister is a simple function of the difference between their ages. Where the gap in time is sufficiently long, an elder girl will already begin to feel the stirring of her maternal instincts towards the helpless newborn baby.

Hostile feelings towards brothers and sisters must be far more frequent in childhood than the unseeing eye of the adult observer can perceive.[17]

In the case of my own children, who followed each other in rapid succession, I neglected the opportunity of carrying out observations of this kind; but I am now making up for this neglect by observing a small nephew, whose autocratic rule was upset, after lasting for fifteen months, by the appearance of a female rival. I am told, it is true, that the young man behaves in the most chivalrous manner to his little sister, that he kisses her hand and strokes her; but I have been able to convince myself that even before the end of his second year he made use of his powers of speech for the purpose of criticizing someone whom he could not fail to regard as superfluous. Whenever the conversation touched upon her he used to intervene in it and exclaim petulantly: 'Too 'ickle! too 'ickle!' During the last few months the baby's growth has made enough progress to place her beyond this particular ground for contempt, and the little boy has found a different basis for his assertion that she does not deserve so much attention: at every suitable opportunity he draws attention to the fact that she has no teeth.[18] We all of us recollect how the eldest girl of another of my sisters, who was then a child of six, spent half an hour in insisting upon each of her aunts in succession agreeing with her: 'Lucie can't understand that yet, can she?' she kept asking. Lucie was her rival – two and a half years her junior.

In none of my women patients, to take an example, have I failed to come upon this dream of the death of a brother or sister, which tallies with an increase in hostility. I have only found a single exception; and it was easy to interpret this as a confirmation of the rule. On one occasion during an analytic session I was explaining this subject to a lady, since in view of her symptom its discussion seemed to me relevant. To my astonishment she replied that she had never had such a dream. Another dream, however, occurred to her, which ostensibly had no connection with the topic – a dream which she had first dreamt when she was four years old and at that time the youngest of the family, and which she had dreamt repeatedly since: *A whole crowd of children – all her brothers, sisters and cousins of both sexes – were romping in a field. Suddenly they all grew wings, flew away and disappeared.* She had no idea what this dream meant; but it is not hard to recognize that in its original form it had been a dream of the death of all her brothers and sisters, and had been only slightly influenced by the censorship. I may venture to suggest the following analysis. On the occasion of the death of one of this crowd of children (in this instance the children of two brothers had been brought up together as a single family) the dreamer, not yet four years old at the time, must have asked some wise grown-up person what became of children when they were dead. The reply must have been: 'They grow wings and turn into little angels.' In the dream which followed upon this piece of information all the dreamer's brothers and sisters had wings like angels and – which is the main point – flew away. Our little baby-killer was left alone, strange to say: the only survivor of the whole crowd! We can hardly be wrong in supposing that the fact of the children romping in a *field* before flying away points to butterflies. It is as though the child was led by the same chain of thought as the peoples of antiquity to picture the soul as having a butterfly's wings.

At this point someone will perhaps interrupt: 'Granted that children have hostile impulses towards their brothers and sisters, how can a child's mind reach such a pitch of depravity as to wish for the *death* of his rivals or of playmates stronger than himself, as though the death penalty were the only punishment for every crime?' Anyone who talks like this has failed to bear in mind that a child's idea of being 'dead' has nothing much in common with ours apart from the word. Children know nothing of the horrors of corruption, of freezing in the ice-cold grave, of the terrors of eternal nothingness – ideas which grown-up people find it so hard to tolerate, as is proved by all the myths of a future life. The fear of death has no meaning to a child; hence it is that he will play with the dreadful word and use it as a threat against a playmate: 'If you do that again, you'll die, like Franz!' Meanwhile the poor mother

Children know nothing of the horrors of corruption, of freezing in the ice-cold grave, of the terrors of eternal nothingness

gives a shudder and remembers, perhaps, that the greater half of the human race fail to survive their childhood years. It was actually possible for a child, who was over eight years old at the time, coming home from a visit to the Natural History Museum, to say to his mother: 'I'm so fond of you, Mummy: when you die I'll have you stuffed and I'll keep you in this room, so that I can see you *all* the time.' So little resemblance is there between a child's idea of being dead and our own![19]

To children, who, moreover, are spared the sight of the scenes of suffering which precede death, being 'dead' means approximately the same as being 'gone' – not troubling the survivors any longer. A child makes no distinction as to how this absence is brought about: whether it is due to a journey, to a dismissal, to an estrangement, or to death.[20] If, during a child's prehistoric epoch, his nurse has been dismissed, and if soon afterwards his mother has died, the two events are superimposed on each other in a single series in his memory as revealed in analysis. When people are absent, children do not miss them with any great intensity; many mothers have learnt this to their sorrow when, after being away from home for some weeks on a summer holiday, they are met on their return by the news that the children have not once asked after their mummy. If their mother does actually make the journey to that 'undiscover'd country, from whose bourn no traveller returns', children seem at first to have forgotten her, and it is only later on that they begin to call their dead mother to mind.

Thus if a child has reasons for wishing the absence of another, there is nothing to restrain him from giving his wish the form of the other child being dead. And the psychical reaction to dreams containing death-wishes proves that, in spite of the different content of these wishes in the case of children, they are nevertheless in some way or other the same as wishes expressed in the same terms by adults.

IF, THEN, A child's death-wishes against his brothers and sisters are explained by the childish egoism which makes him regard them as his rivals, how are we to explain his death-wishes against his parents, who surround him with love and fulfil his needs and whose preservation that same egoism should lead him to desire?

A solution of this difficulty is afforded by the observation that dreams of the death of parents apply with preponderant frequency to the parent who is of the same sex as the dreamer: that men, that is, dream mostly of their father's death and women of their mother's. I cannot pretend that this is universally so, but the preponderance in the direction I have indicated is so evident that it requires to be explained by a factor of general importance.[21] It is as though – to put it bluntly – a sexual preference were making itself felt at an early age: as though boys regarded their fathers and girls their mothers as their rivals in love, whose elimination could not fail to be to their advantage.

Before this idea is rejected as a monstrous one, it is as well in this case, too, to consider the real relations obtaining – this time between parents and children. We must distinguish between what the cultural standards of filial piety demand of this relation and what everyday observation shows it in fact to be. More than one occasion for hostility lies concealed in the relation between parents and children – a relation which affords the most ample opportunities for wishes to arise which cannot pass the censorship.

Let us consider first the relation between father and son. The sanctity which we attribute to the rules laid down in the Decalogue has, I think, blunted our powers of perceiving the real facts. We seem scarcely to venture to observe that the majority of mankind disobey the Fifth Commandment. Alike in the lowest and in the highest strata of human society filial piety is wont to give way to other interests. The obscure information which is brought to us by mythology and legend from the primaeval ages of human society gives an unpleasing picture of the father's despotic power and of the ruthlessness with which he made use of it. Kronos devoured his children, just as the wild boar devours the sow's litter; while Zeus emasculated his father[22] and made himself ruler in his place. The more unrestricted was the rule of the father in the ancient family, the more must the son, as his destined successor, have found himself in the position of an enemy, and the more impatient must he have been to become ruler himself through his father's death. Even in our middle-class families fathers are as a rule inclined to refuse their sons independence and the means necessary to secure it and thus to foster the growth of the germ of hostility which is inherent in their relation. A physician will often be in a position to notice how a son's grief at the loss of his father cannot suppress his satisfaction at having at length won his freedom. In our society to-day fathers are apt to cling desperately to what is left of a now sadly antiquated *potestas patris familias*; and an author who, like Ibsen, brings the immemorial struggle between fathers and sons into prominence in his writings may be certain of producing his effect.

Occasions for conflict between a daughter and her mother arise when the daughter begins to grow up and long for sexual liberty, but finds herself under her mother's tutelage; while the mother, on the other hand, is warned by her daughter's growth that the time has come when she herself must abandon her claims to sexual satisfaction.

All of this is patent to the eyes of everyone. But it does not help us in our endeavour to explain dreams of a parent's death in people whose piety towards their parents has long been unimpeachably established. Previous discussions, moreover, will have prepared us to learn that the death-wish against parents dates back to earliest childhood.

This supposition is confirmed with a certainty beyond

all doubt in the case of psychoneurotics when they are subjected to analysis. We learn from them that a child's sexual wishes – if in their embryonic stage they deserve to be so described – awaken very early, and that a girl's first affection is for her father[23] and a boy's first childish desires are for his mother. Accordingly, the father becomes a disturbing rival to the boy and the mother to the girl; and I have already shown in the case of brothers and sisters how easily such feelings can lead to a death-wish. The parents too give evidence as a rule of sexual partiality: a natural predilection usually sees to it that a man tends to spoil his little daughters, while his wife takes her sons' part; though both of them, where their judgement is not disturbed by the magic of sex, keep a strict eye upon their children's education. The child is very well aware of this partiality and turns against that one of his parents who is opposed to showing it. Being loved by an adult does not merely bring a child the satisfaction of a special need; it also means that he will get what he wants in every other respect as well. Thus he will be following his own sexual instinct and at the same time giving fresh strength to the inclination shown by his parents if his choice between them falls in with theirs.

The signs of these infantile preferences are for the most part overlooked; yet some of them are to be observed even after the first years of childhood. An eight-year-old girl of my acquaintance, if her mother is called away from the table, makes use of the occasion to proclaim herself her successor: 'I'm going to be Mummy now. Do you want some more greens, Karl? Well, help yourself, then!' and so on. A particularly gifted and lively girl of four, in whom this piece of child psychology is especially transparent, declared quite openly: 'Mummy can go away now. Then Daddy must marry me and I'll be his wife.' Such a wish occurring in a child is not in the least inconsistent with her being tenderly attached to her mother. If a little boy is allowed to sleep beside his mother when his father is away from home, but has to go back to the nursery and to some-one of whom he is far less fond as soon as his father returns, he may easily begin to form a wish that his father should *always* be away, so that he himself could keep his place beside his dear, lovely Mummy. One obvious way of attaining this wish would be if his father were dead; for the child has learnt one thing by experience – namely that 'dead' people, such as Grandaddy, are always away and never come back.

THOUGH OBSERVATIONS OF this kind on small children fit in perfectly with the interpretation I have proposed, they do not carry such complete conviction as is forced upon the physician by psycho-analyses of adult neurotics. In the latter case dreams of the sort we are considering are introduced into the analysis in such a context that it is impossible to avoid interpreting them as *wishful* dreams.

One day one of my women patients was in a distressed and tearful mood. 'I don't want ever to see my relations again,' she said, 'they must think me horrible.' She then went on, with almost no transition, to say that she remembered a dream, though of course she had no idea what it meant. When she was four years old she had a dream that *a lynx or fox*[24] *was walking on the roof; then something had fallen down or she had fallen down; and then her mother was carried out of the house dead* – and she wept bitterly. I told her that this dream must mean that when she was a child she had wished she could see her mother dead, and that it must be on account of the dream that she felt her relations must think her horrible. I had scarcely said this when she produced some material which threw light on the dream. 'Lynx-eye' was a term of abuse that had been thrown at her by a street-urchin when she was a very small child. When she was three years old, a tile off the roof had fallen on her mother's head and made it bleed violently.

I once had an opportunity of making a detailed study of a young woman who passed through a variety of psychical conditions. Her illness began with a state of confusional excitement during which she displayed a quite special aversion to her mother, hitting and abusing her whenever she came near her bed, while at the same period she was docile and affectionate towards a sister who was many years her senior. This was followed by a state in which she was lucid but somewhat apathetic and suffered from badly disturbed sleep. It was during this phase that I began treating her and analysing her dreams. An immense number of these dreams were concerned, with a greater or less degree of disguise, with the death of her mother: at one time she would be attending an old woman's funeral, at another she and her sister would be sitting at table dressed in mourning. There could be no question as to the meaning of these dreams. As her condition improved still further, hysterical phobias developed. The most tormenting of these was a fear that something might have happened to her mother. She was obliged to hurry home, wherever she might be, to convince herself that her mother was still alive. This case, taken in conjunction with what I had learnt from other sources, was highly instructive: it exhibited, translated as it were into different languages, the various ways in which the psychical apparatus reacted to one and the same exciting idea. In the confusional state, in which, as I believe, the second psychical agency was overwhelmed by the normally suppressed first one, her unconscious hostility to her mother found a powerful *motor* expression. When the calmer condition set in, when the rebellion was suppressed and the domination of the censorship re-established, the only region left open in which her hostility could realize the wish for her mother's death was that of dreaming. When a normal state was still more firmly established, it led to the production of her exaggerated worry about her mother as a hysterical counter-reaction and defensive phenomenon. In view of this it is no longer hard to understand why hysterical girls are so often attached to their mothers with such exaggerated affection.

On another occasion I had an opportunity of obtaining a deep insight into the unconscious mind of a young man whose life was made almost impossible by an obsessional neurosis. He was unable to go out into the street because he was tortured by the fear that he would kill everyone he met. He spent his days in preparing his alibi in case he might be charged with one of the murders committed in the town. It is unnecessary to add that he was a man of equally high morals and education. The analysis (which, incidentally, led to his recovery) showed that the basis of this distressing obsession was an impulse to murder his somewhat over-severe father. This impulse, to his astonishment, had been consciously expressed when he was seven years old, but it had, of course, originated much earlier in his childhood. After his father's painful illness and death, the patient's obsessional self-reproaches appeared – he was in his thirty-first year at the time – taking the shape of a phobia transferred on to strangers. A person, he felt, who was capable of wanting to push his own father over a precipice from the top of a mountain was not to be trusted to respect the lives of those less closely related to him; he was quite right to shut himself up in his room.

IN MY EXPERIENCE, which is already extensive, the chief part in the mental lives of all children who later become psychoneurotics is played by their parents. Being in love with the one parent and hating the other are among the essential constituents of the stock of psychical impulses which is formed at that time and which is of such importance in determining the symptoms of the later neurosis. It is not my belief, however, that psychoneurotics differ sharply in this respect from other human beings who remain normal – that they are able, that is, to create something absolutely new and peculiar to themselves. It is far more probable – and this is confirmed by occasional observations on normal children – that they are only distinguished by exhibiting on a magnified scale feelings of love and hatred to their parents which occur less obviously and less intensely in the minds of most children.

This discovery is confirmed by a legend that has come down to us from classical antiquity: a legend whose profound and universal power to move can only be understood if the hypothesis I have put forward in regard to the psychology of children has an equally universal validity. What I have in mind is the legend of King Oedipus and Sophocles' drama which bears his name.

Oedipus, son of Laïus, King of Thebes, and of Jocasta, was exposed as an infant because an oracle had warned Laïus that the still unborn child would be his father's murderer. The child was rescued, and grew up as a prince in an alien court, until, in doubts as to his origin, he too questioned the oracle and was warned to avoid his home since he was destined to murder his father and take his mother in marriage. On the road leading away from what he believed was his home, he met King Laïus and slew him in a sudden quarrel. He came next to Thebes and solved the riddle set him by the Sphinx who barred his way. Out of gratitude the Thebans made him their king and gave him Jocasta's hand in marriage. He reigned long in peace and honour, and she who, unknown to him, was his mother bore him two sons and two daughters. Then at last a plague broke out and the Thebans made enquiry once more of the oracle. It is at this point that Sophocles' tragedy opens. The messengers bring back the reply that the plague will cease when the murderer of Laïus has been driven from the land.

> But he, where is he? Where shall now be read
> The fading record of this ancient guilt?

The action of the play consists in nothing other than the process of revealing, with cunning delays and ever-mounting excitement – a process that can be likened to the work of a psychoanalysis – that Oedipus himself is the murderer of Laïus, but further that he is the son of the murdered man and of Jocasta. Appalled at the abomination which he has unwittingly perpetrated, Oedipus blinds himself and forsakes his home. The oracle has been fulfilled.

Oedipus Rex is what is known as a tragedy of destiny. Its tragic effect is said to lie in the contrast between the supreme will of the gods and the vain attempts of mankind to escape the evil that threatens them. The lesson which, it is said, the deeply moved spectator should learn from the tragedy is submission to the divine will and realization of his own impotence. Modern dramatists have accordingly tried to achieve a similar tragic effect by weaving the same contrast into a plot invented by themselves. But the spectators have looked on unmoved while a curse or an oracle was fulfilled in spite of all the efforts of some innocent man: later tragedies of destiny have failed in their effect.

If *Oedipus Rex* moves a modern audience no less than it did the contemporary Greek one, the explanation can only be that its effect does not lie in the contrast between destiny and human will, but is to be looked for in the particular nature of the material on which that contrast is exemplified. There must be something which makes a voice within us ready to recognize the compelling force of destiny in the *Oedipus*, while we can dismiss as merely arbitrary such dispositions as are laid down in [Grillparzer's] *Die Ahnfrau* or other modern tragedies of destiny. And a factor of this kind is in fact involved in the story of King Oedipus. His destiny moves us only because it might have been ours – because the oracle laid the same curse upon us before our birth as upon him. It is the fate of all of us, perhaps, to direct our first sexual impulse towards our mother and our first hatred and our first murderous wish against our father. Our dreams convince us that that is so. King Oedipus, who slew his father Laïus and married his mother Jocasta, merely shows us the fulfilment of our own childhood wishes. But, more fortunate than he, we have meanwhile succeeded, in so far as we have not become psychoneurotics, in detaching our sexual impulses from our mothers and in forgetting our jealousy of our fathers. Here is one in whom these primaeval wishes of our childhood have been fulfilled, and we shrink back from him with the whole force of the repression by which those wishes have since that time been held down within us. While the poet, as he unravels the past, brings to light the guilt of Oedipus, he is at the same time compelling us to recognize our own inner minds, in which those same impulses, though suppressed, are still to be found. The contrast with which the closing Chorus leaves us confronted –

> . . . Fix on Oedipus your eyes,
> Who resolved the dark enigma, noblest champion and most wise.
> Like a star his envied fortune mounted beaming far and wide:
> Now he sinks in seas of anguish, whelmed beneath a raging tide . . .

– strikes as a warning at ourselves and our pride, at us who since our childhood have grown so wise and so mighty in our own eyes. Like Oedipus, we live in ignorance of these wishes, repugnant to morality, which have been forced upon us by Nature, and after their revelation we may all of us well seek to close our eyes to the scenes of our childhood.[25]

There is an unmistakable indication in the text of Sophocles' tragedy itself that the legend of Oedipus sprang from some primaeval dream-material which had as its content the distressing disturbance of a child's relation to his parents owing to the first stirrings of sexuality. At a point when Oedipus, though he is not yet enlightened, has begun to feel troubled by his recollection of the oracle, Jocasta consoles him by referring to a dream which many people dream, though, as she thinks, it has no meaning:

> Many a man ere now in dreams hath lain
> With her who bare him. He hath least annoy
> Who with such omens troubleth not his mind.

To-day, just as then, many men dream of having sexual relations with their mothers, and speak of the fact with indignation and astonishment. It is clearly the key to the tragedy and the complement to the dream of the dreamer's father being dead. The story of Oedipus is the reaction of the imagination to these two typical dreams. And just as these dreams, when dreamt by adults, are accompanied by feelings of repulsion, so too the legend must include horror and self-punishment. Its further modification originates once again in a misconceived secondary revision of the material, which has sought to exploit it for theological purposes. (Cf. the dream-material in dreams of exhibiting, p. 82 f.) The attempt to harmonize divine omnipotence with human responsibility must naturally

Many men dream of having sexual relations with their mothers, and speak of the fact with indignation and astonishment

fail in connection with this subject-matter just as with any other.

ANOTHER OF THE great creations of tragic poetry, Shakespeare's *Hamlet*, has its roots in the same soil as *Oedipus Rex*. But the changed treatment of the same material reveals the whole difference in the mental life of these two widely separated epochs of civilization: the secular advance of repression in the emotional life of mankind. In the *Oedipus* the child's wishful phantasy that underlies it is brought into the open and realized as it would be in a dream. In *Hamlet* it remains repressed; and – just as in the case of a neurosis – we only learn of its existence from its inhibiting consequences. Strangely enough, the overwhelming effect produced by the more modern tragedy has turned out to be compatible with the fact that people have remained completely in the dark as to the hero's character. The play is built up on Hamlet's hesitations over fulfilling the task of revenge that is assigned to him; but its text offers no reasons or motives for these hesitations and an immense variety of attempts at interpreting them have failed to produce a result. According to the view which was originated by Goethe and is still the prevailing one to-day, Hamlet represents the type of man whose power of direct action is paralysed by an excessive development of his intellect. (He is 'sicklied o'er with the pale cast of thought'.) According to another view, the dramatist has tried to portray a pathologically

irresolute character which might be classed as neuras-
thenic. The plot of the drama shows us, however, that
Hamlet is far from being represented as a person incapable of taking any action. We see him doing so on two
occasions: first in a sudden outburst of temper, when he
runs his sword through the eavesdropper behind the
arras, and secondly in a premeditated and even crafty
fashion, when, with all the callousness of a Renaissance
prince, he sends the two courtiers to the death that had
been planned for himself. What is it, then, that inhibits
him in fulfilling the task set him by his father's ghost? The
answer, once again, is that it is the peculiar nature of the
task. Hamlet is able to do anything – except take ven-
geance on the man who did away with his father and took
that father's place with his mother, the man who shows
him the repressed wishes of his own childhood realized.
Thus the loathing which should drive him on to revenge
is replaced in him by self-reproaches, by scruples of con-
science, which remind him that he himself is literally no
better than the sinner whom he is to punish. Here I have
translated into conscious terms what was bound to
remain unconscious in Hamlet's mind; and if anyone is
inclined to call him a hysteric, I can only accept the fact
as one that is implied by my interpretation. The distaste
for sexuality expressed by Hamlet in his conversation
with Ophelia fits in very well with this: the same distaste
which was destined to take possession of the poet's mind
more and more during the years that followed, and which

reached its extreme expression in *Timon of Athens*. For it can of course only be the poet's own mind which confronts us in Hamlet. I observe in a book on Shakespeare by Georg Brandes (1896) a statement that *Hamlet* was written immediately after the death of Shakespeare's father (in 1601), that is, under the immediate impact of his bereavement and, as we may well assume, while his childhood feelings about his father had been freshly revived. It is known, too, that Shakespeare's own son who died at an early age bore the name of 'Hamnet', which is identical with 'Hamlet'. Just as *Hamlet* deals with the relation of a son to his parents, so *Macbeth* (written at approximately the same period) is concerned with the subject of childlessness. But just as all neurotic symptoms, and, for that matter, dreams, are capable of being 'over-interpreted' and indeed need to be, if they are to be fully understood, so all genuinely creative writings are the product of more than a single motive and more than a single impulse in the poet's mind, and are open to more than a single interpretation. In what I have written I have only attempted to interpret the deepest layer of impulses in the mind of the creative writer.[26]

I CANNOT LEAVE the subject of typical dreams of the death of loved relatives, without adding a few more words to throw light on their significance for the theory of dreams in general. In these dreams we find the highly unusual condition realized of a dream-thought formed by a repressed wish entirely eluding censorship and passing into the dream without modification. There must be special factors at work to make this event possible, and I believe that the occurrence of these dreams is facilitated by two such factors. Firstly, there is no wish that seems more remote from us than this one: 'we couldn't even *dream*' – so we believe – of wishing such a thing. For this reason the dream-censorship is not armed to meet such a monstrosity, just as Solon's penal code contained no punishment for parricide. Secondly, in this case the repressed and unsuspected wish is particularly often met half-way by a residue from the previous day in the form of a *worry* about the safety of the person concerned. This worry can only make its way into the dream by availing itself of the corresponding wish; while the wish can disguise itself behind the worry that has become active during the day.[27] We may feel inclined to think that things are simpler than this and that one merely carries on during the night and in dreams with what one has been turning over in one's mind during the day; but if so we shall be leaving dreams of the death of people of whom the dreamer is fond completely in the air and without any connection with our explanation of dreams in general, and we shall thus be clinging quite unnecessarily to a riddle which is perfectly capable of solution.

It is also instructive to consider the relation of these dreams to anxiety-dreams. In the dreams we have been discussing, a repressed wish has found a means of evading censorship – and the distortion which censorship involves. The invariable concomitant is that painful feelings are experienced in the dream. In just the same way anxiety-dreams only occur if the censorship has been wholly or partly overpowered; and, on the other hand, the over-powering of the censorship is facilitated if anxiety has already been produced as an immediate sensation arising from somatic sources.[28] We can thus plainly see the pur-pose for which the censorship exercises its office and brings about the distortion of dreams: it does so *in order to prevent the generation of anxiety or other forms of distressing affect.*

I HAVE SPOKEN above [p. 92] of the egoism of children's minds, and I may now add, with a hint at a possible connection between the two facts, that dreams have the same characteristic. All of them are completely egoistic: the beloved ego appears in all of them, even though it may be disguised. The wishes that are fulfilled in them are invariably the ego's wishes, and if a dream seems to have been provoked by an altruistic interest, we are only being deceived by appearances. Here are a few analyses of instances which seem to contradict this assertion.

I

A child of under four years old reported having dreamt that *he had seen a big dish with a big joint of roast meat and vegetables on it. All at once the joint had been eaten up – whole and without being cut up. He had not seen the person who ate it.*

Who can the unknown person have been whose sumptuous banquet of meat was the subject of the little boy's dream? His experiences during the dream-day must enlighten us on the subject. By doctor's orders he had been put on a milk diet for the past few days. On the evening of the dream-day he had been naughty, and as a punishment he had been sent to bed without his supper. He had been through this hunger-cure once before and had been very brave about it. He knew he would get nothing, but would not allow himself to show by so much as a single word that he was hungry. Education had already begun to have an effect on him: it found expression in this dream, which exhibits the beginning of dream-distortion. There can be no doubt that the person whose wishes were aimed at this lavish meal – a meat meal, too – was himself. But since he knew he was not allowed it, he did not venture to sit down to the meal himself, as hungry children do in dreams.[29] The person who ate the meal remained anonymous.

II

I dreamt one night that I saw in the window of a book-shop a new volume in one of the series of monographs for connoisseurs which I am in the habit of buying – monographs on great artists, on world history, on famous cities, etc. *The new series was called 'Famous Speakers' or 'Speeches' and its first volume bore the name of Dr. Lecher.*

When I came to analyse this, it seemed to me improbable that I should be concerned in my dreams with the fame of Dr. Lecher, the non-stop speaker of the German Nationalist obstructionists in Parliament. The position was that a few days earlier I had taken on some new patients for psychological treatment, and was now obliged to talk for ten or eleven hours every day. So it was I myself who was a non-stop speaker.

III

Another time I had a dream that a man I knew on the staff of the University said to me: *'My son, the Myops.'* Then followed a dialogue made up of short remarks and rejoinders. After this, however, there was yet a third piece of dream in which I myself and my sons figured. So far as the dream's latent content was concerned, Professor M. and his son were men of straw – a mere screen for me and my eldest son. I shall have to return to this dream later, on account of another of its features.[30]

IV

The dream which follows is an instance of really low egoistic feelings concealed behind affectionate worry.

My friend Otto was looking ill. His face was brown and he had protruding eyes.

Otto is my family doctor, and I owe him more than I can ever hope to repay: he has watched over my children's health for many years, he has treated them successfully when they have been ill, and, in addition, whenever circumstances have given him an excuse, he has given them presents.[31] He had visited us on the dream-day, and my wife had remarked that he looked tired and strained. That night I had my dream, which showed him with some of the signs of Basedow's [Graves'] disease. Anyone who interprets this dream without regard for my rules will conclude that I was worried about my friend's health and that this worry was realized in the dream. This would not only contradict my assertion that dreams are wish-fulfilments, but my other assertion, too, that they are accessible only to egoistic impulses. But I should be glad if anyone interpreting the dream in this way would be good enough to explain to me why my fears on Otto's behalf should have lighted on *Basedow's* disease – a diagnosis for which his actual appearance gives not the slightest ground. My analysis, on the other hand, brought up the following material from an occurrence six years earlier. A small group of us, which included Professor R., were driving in pitch darkness through the forest of N., which lay some hours' drive from the place at which we were spending our summer holidays. The coachman, who was not perfectly sober, spilt us, carriage and all, over an embankment, and it was only by a piece of luck that we all escaped injury. We were obliged, however, to spend the night in a neighbouring inn, at which the news of our accident brought us a lot of sympathy. A gentleman, with unmistakable signs of Basedow's disease – incidentally, just as in the dream, only the brown discoloration of the skin of the face and the protruding eyes, but no goitre – placed himself entirely at our disposal and asked what he could do for us. Professor R. replied in his decisive manner: 'Nothing except to lend me a night-shirt.' To which the fine gentleman rejoined: 'I'm sorry, but I can't do that', and left the room.

As I continued my analysis, it occurred to me that Basedow was the name not only of a physician but also of a famous educationalist. (In my waking state I no longer felt quite so certain about this.[32]) But my friend Otto was the person whom I had asked to watch over my children's physical education, especially at the age of puberty (hence the night-shirt), in case anything happened to me. By giving my friend Otto in the dream the symptoms of our noble helper, I was evidently saying that if anything happened to me he would do just as little for the children as Baron L. had done on that occasion in spite of his kind offers of assistance. This seems to be sufficient evidence of the egoistic lining of the dream.[33]

But where was its wish-fulfilment to be found? Not in my avenging myself on my friend Otto, whose fate it seems to be to be ill-treated in my dreams; but in the following consideration. At the same time as I represented Otto in the dream as Baron L., I had identified myself with someone else, namely Professor R.; for just as in the anecdote R. had made a request to Baron L., so I had made a request to Otto. And that is the point. Professor R., with whom I should really not venture to compare myself in the ordinary way, resembled me in having followed an independent path outside the academic world and had only achieved his well-merited title late in life. So once again I was wanting to be a Professor! Indeed the words 'late in life' were themselves a wish-fulfilment; for they implied that I should live long enough to see my boys through the age of puberty myself.[34]

(γ) Other Typical Dreams

I have no experience of my own of other kinds of typical dreams, in which the dreamer finds himself flying through the air to the accompaniment of agreeable feelings or falling with feelings of anxiety; and whatever I have to say on the subject is derived from psycho-analyses. The information provided by the latter forces me to conclude that these dreams, too, reproduce impressions of childhood; they relate, that is, to games involving movement, which are extraordinarily attractive to children. There cannot be a single uncle who has not shown a child how to fly by rushing across the room with him in his outstretched arms, or who has not played at letting him fall by riding him on his knee and then suddenly stretching out his leg, or by holding him up high and then suddenly pretending to drop him. Children are delighted by such experiences and never tire of asking to have them repeated, especially if there is something about them that causes a little fright or giddiness. In after years they repeat these experiences in dreams; but in the dreams they leave out the hands which held them up, so that they float or fall unsupported. The delight taken by young children in games of this kind (as well as in swings and see-saws) is well known; and when they come to see acrobatic feats in a circus their memory of such games is revived.[35] Hysterical attacks in boys sometimes consist merely in reproductions of feats of this kind, carried out with great skill. It not uncommonly happens that these games of movement, though innocent in themselves, give rise to sexual feelings.[36] Childish 'romping' ['Hetzen'], if I may use a word which commonly describes all such activities, is what is being repeated in dreams of flying, falling, giddiness and so on; while the pleasurable feelings attached to these experiences are transformed into anxiety. But often enough, as every mother knows, romping among children actually ends in squabbling and tears.

THE TRUTH IN the assertion made in the text above is thus restricted to the fact that among the unconscious instigators of a dream we very frequently find egoistic impulses which seem to have been overcome in waking life.

Thus I have good grounds for rejecting the theory that what provokes dreams of flying and falling is the state of our tactile feelings during sleep or sensations of the movement of our lungs, and so on.[37] In my view these sensations are themselves reproduced as part of the memory to which the dream goes back: that is to say, they are part of the *content* of the dream and not its source.

I cannot, however, disguise from myself that I am unable to produce any complete explanation of this class of typical dreams. My material has left me in the lurch precisely at this point. I must, however, insist upon the general assertion that all the tactile and motor sensations which occur in these typical dreams are called up immediately there is any psychical reason for making use of them and that they can be disregarded when no such need for them arises.[38] I am also of the opinion that the relation of these dreams to infantile experiences has been established with certainty from the indications I have found in the analyses of psychoneurotics. I am not able to say, however, what other meanings may become attached to the recollection of such sensations in the course of later life – different meanings, perhaps, in every individual case, in spite of the typical appearance of the dreams; and I should be glad to be able to fill up the gap by a careful analysis of clear instances. If anyone feels surprised that, in spite of the frequency precisely of dreams of flying, falling and pulling out teeth, etc., I should be complaining of lack of material on this particular topic, I must explain that I myself have not experienced any dreams of the kind since I turned my attention to the subject of dream-interpretation. The dreams of neurotics, moreover, of which I might otherwise avail myself, cannot always be interpreted – not, at least, in many cases, so as to reveal the whole of their concealed meaning; a particular psychical force, which was concerned with the original constructing of the neurosis and is brought into operation once again when attempts are made at resolving it, prevents us from interpreting such dreams down to their last secret.

(δ) Examination Dreams

Everyone who has passed the matriculation examination at the end of his school studies complains of the obstinacy with which he is pursued by anxiety-dreams of having failed, or of being obliged to take the examination again, etc. In the case of those who have obtained a University degree this typical dream is replaced by another one which represents them as having failed in their University Finals; and it is in vain that they object, even while they are still asleep, that for years they have been practising medicine or working as University lecturers or heads of offices. The ineradicable memories of the punishments that we suffered for our evil deeds in childhood become active within us once more and attach themselves to the two crucial points in our studies – the *'dies irae, dies illa'* of our stiffest examinations. The 'examination anxiety' of neurotics owes its intensification to these same childhood fears. After we have ceased to be school-children, our punishments are no longer inflicted on us by our parents or by those who brought us up or later by our school-masters. The relentless causal chains of real life take charge of our further education, and now we dream of Matriculation or Finals (and who has not trembled on those occasions, even if he was well-prepared for the examination?) whenever, having done something wrong or failed to do something properly, we expect to be punished by the event – whenever, in short, we feel the burden of responsibility.

For a further explanation of examination dreams I have to thank an experienced colleague [Stekel], who once declared at a scientific meeting that so far as he knew dreams of Matriculation only occur in people who have successfully passed it and never in people who have failed in it. It would seem, then, that anxious examination dreams (which, as has been confirmed over and over again, appear when the dreamer has some responsible activity ahead of him next day and is afraid there may be a fiasco) search for some occasion in the past in which great anxiety has turned out to be unjustified and has been contradicted by the event. This, then, would be a very striking instance of the content of a dream being misunderstood by the waking agency. [See p. 83] What is regarded as an indignant protest against the dream: 'But I'm a doctor, etc., already!' would in reality be the consolation put forward by the dream, and would accordingly run: 'Don't be afraid of tomorrow! Just think how anxious you were before your Matriculation, and yet nothing happened to you. You're a doctor, etc., already.' And the anxiety which is attributed to the dream would really have arisen from the day's residues.

Such tests as I have been able to make of this explanation on myself and on other people, though they have not been sufficiently numerous, have confirmed its validity. For instance, I myself failed in Forensic Medicine in my Finals; but I have never had to cope with this subject in dreams, whereas I have quite often been examined in Botany, Zoology or Chemistry. I went in for the examination in these subjects with well-founded anxiety; but, whether by the grace of destiny or of the examiners, I escaped punishment. In my dreams of school examinations, I am invariably examined in History, in which I did brilliantly – though only, it is true, because [in the oral examination] my kindly master (the one-eyed benefactor of another dream[39] did not fail to notice that on the paper of questions which I handed him back I had run my finger-nail through the middle one of the three questions included, to warn him not to insist upon that particular one. One of my patients, who decided not to sit for his Matriculation the first time but passed it later, and who subsequently failed in his army examination and never got a commission, has told me that he often dreams of the former of these examinations but never of the latter.

The interpretation of examination dreams is faced by the difficulty which I have already referred to as characteristic of the majority of typical dreams [p. 79]. It is but rarely that the material with which the dreamer provides us in associations is sufficient to interpret the dream. It is only by collecting a considerable number of examples of such dreams that we can arrive at a better understanding of them. Not long ago I came to the conclusion that the objection, 'You're a doctor, etc., already', does not merely conceal a consolation but also signifies a reproach. This would have run: 'You're quite old now, quite far advanced in life, and yet you go on doing these stupid, childish things.' This mixture of self-criticism and consolation would thus correspond to the latent content of examination dreams. If so, it would not be surprising if the self-reproaches for being 'stupid' and 'childish' in these last examples referred to the repetition of reprehensible sexual acts.

Wilhelm Stekel, who put forward the first interpretation of dreams of Matriculation ['*Matura*'], was of the opinion that they regularly related to sexual tests and sexual maturity. My experience has often confirmed his view.

Notes

On Dreams

1. The German original appeared in the series *Grundfragen des Nerven- und Seelenlebens*, published by Bergmann (Wiesbaden). The present translation is included in *Standard Ed.*, 5, 633.

2. [These lines are from one of the Harp-player's songs in Goethe's *Wilhelm Meister*. In the original the words are addressed to the Heavenly Powers and may be translated literally: 'You lead us into life, you make the poor creature guilty.' But the words '*Armen*' and '*schuldig*' are both capable of bearing another meaning. '*Armen*' might mean 'poor' in the financial sense and '*schuldig*' might mean 'in debt'. So in the present context the last line could be rendered: 'You make the poor man fall into debt.']

3. [The first line of the couplet might now be taken to mean that the verses are addressed to parents.]

4. [Most of these dreams are reported in greater detail in *The Interpretation of Dreams* (1900a), *Standard Ed.*, 4, 122 ff.; *P.F.L.*, 4, 200 ff.; and in Lecture 8 of the *Introductory Lectures* (1916–17), *Standard Ed.*, 15, 126 ff; *P.F.L.*, 1, 157 ff.]

5. [The German word '*Kosten*' means both 'cost' and 'to taste'.]

6. [The '*trottoir roulant*' was a moving roadway installed at the Paris Exhibition of 1900.]

7. ['If you go hat in hand, you can cross the whole land.']

8. [This should probably be 'red'. The flowers are so described in the much fuller account of the dream given in *The Interpretation of Dreams* (*Standard Ed.*, 5, 347, *P.F.L.*, 4, 463f.).]

9. [A ceremonial portico on the Athenian model.]

10. [*Footnote added* 1911:] It deserves to be remarked that well-known philologists have asserted that the most ancient human languages tended in general to express contradictory opposites by the same word. (E.g. 'strong-weak', 'inside-outside'. This has been described as 'the antithetical meaning of primal words'.) [Cf. Freud, 1910e.]

11. [A reference to Wilhelm Fliess (1858–1928), an otolaryngologist with whom Freud, early in his career, conducted an extensive correspondence (Freud, 1950a). Cf. Fliess (1892).]

12. [Freud has, however, qualified this statement in an additional footnote written in 1925, which will be found near the end of Chapter V of *The Interpretation of Dreams* (See 'Typical Dreams', footnote 20).]

13. ['*Schafkopf*', literally 'sheep's head' = 'silly ass'.]

14. ['This was written by no Goethe, this was composed by no Schiller.']

15. See my *Three Essays on the Theory of Sexuality* (1905d). [Chapter 5 in *Standard Ed.*, 4]

16. [See, however, the qualification three paragraphs lower down.]

17. Cf. '*Frauenzimmer*' [literally 'women's apartment,' commonly used in German as a slightly derogatory word for 'woman'].

18. Further information on dream-symbolism may be found in the works of early writers on dream-interpretation, e.g. Artemidorus of Daldis and Scherner (1861), and also in my own *Interpretation of Dreams* (1900a) [Chapter VI, Section E], in the mythological studies of the psychoanalytic school, as well as in some of W. Stekel's writings (e.g. 1911).

Typical Dreams

1. [*Footnote added* 1925:] This assertion that our method of interpreting dreams cannot be applied unless we have access to the dreamer's associative material requires supplementing: our interpretative activity is in one instance independent of these associations – if, namely, the dreamer has employed *symbolic* elements in the content of the dream. In such cases we make use of what is, strictly speaking, a second and auxiliary method of dream-interpretation. (See *Standard Ed.*, 5, 359 f.)

2. [See ibid., 5, 351 ff.]

3. [See ibid., 384 ff.]

4. [German playwright, 1862–1939.]

5. A child plays a part in the fairy tale as well; for it was a small child who suddenly exclaimed: 'But he has nothing on!'

6. [See *Standard Ed.*, 4, 218]

7. [*Footnote added* 1911:] Ferenczi [1910] has recorded a number of interesting dreams of being naked dreamt by *women*. There was no difficulty in tracing these back to the infantile desire to exhibit; but they differed in some respects from the 'typical' dreams of being naked which I have discussed in the text. – [The penultimate sentence in the paragraph above

seems to adumbrate some of the ideas put forward twenty
years later in *Beyond the Pleasure Principle* (Freud, 1920*g*).]

8. [See *Standard Ed.*, 4, 335 ff.]

9. [See ibid., 238]

10. [See ibid., 314]

11. Here is an 'over-interpretation' of the same dream. Since
    '*spuken* [haunting]' is an activity of *spirits*, '*spucken* [spit-
    ting] on the stairs' might be loosely rendered as '*esprit
    d'escalier*'. This last phrase is equivalent to lack of ready rep-
    artee ['*Schlagfertigkeit*', literally 'readiness to strike'] – a
    failing to which I must in fact plead guilty. Was my nurse, I
    wonder, equally wanting in that quality? [This nurse is
    referred to at the end of Chapter IV of *The Psychopathology
    of Everyday Life* (Freud, 1901*b*) and in greater detail in his
    letters to Fliess of October 3 and 4 and October 15, 1897
    (Freud, 1950*a*, Letters 70 and 71).]

12. (See *Standard Ed.*, 4, 152)

13. (See ibid., 154)

14. [*Footnote added* 1909:] Cf. my 'Analysis of a Phobia in a Five-
    Year-Old Boy' (1909*b*) and my paper 'On the Sexual Theories
    of Children' (1908*c*).

15. [*Footnote added* 1909:] The three-and-a-half-year-old Hans
    (whose phobia was the subject of the analysis mentioned in
    the preceding footnote) exclaimed shortly after the birth of
    a sister, while he was suffering from a feverish sore throat: 'I
    don't *want* a baby sister!' [Freud, 1909*b*, Section I.] During
    his neurosis eighteen months later he frankly confessed to a
    wish that his mother might drop the baby into the bath so
    that she would die. [Ibid., Section II (April 11).] At the same
    time, Hans was a good-natured and affectionate child, who
    soon grew fond of this same sister and particularly enjoyed
    taking her under his wing.

16. [*Footnote added* 1914:] Deaths that are experienced in this way in childhood may quickly be forgotten in the family; but psycho-analytic research shows that they have a very important influence on subsequent neuroses.

17. [*Footnote added* 1914:] Since this was written, a large number of observations have been made and recorded in the literature of psychoanalysis upon the originally hostile attitude of children towards their brothers and sisters and one of their parents. The [Swiss] author and poet Spitteler has given us a particularly genuine and naïve account of this childish attitude, derived from his own childhood [1914, 40]: 'Moreover there was a second Adolf there: a little creature who they alleged was my brother, though I could not see what use he was and still less why they made as much fuss of him as of me myself. I was sufficient so far as I was concerned; why should I want a brother? And he was not merely useless, he was positively in the way. When I pestered my grandmother, he wanted to pester her too. When I was taken out in the perambulator, he sat opposite to me and took up half the space, so that we were bound to kick each other with our feet.'

18. [*Footnote added* 1909:] Little Hans, when he was three and a half, gave vent to a crushing criticism of his sister in the same words. It was because of her lack of teeth, he supposed, that she was unable to talk. [Freud, 1909b, Section I.]

19. [*Footnote added* 1909:] I was astonished to hear a highly intelligent boy of ten remark after the sudden death of his father: 'I know father's dead, but what I can't understand is why he doesn't come home to supper.' – [*Added* 1919:] Further material on this subject will be found in the first [seven] volumes of the periodical *Imago* [1912–21], under the standing rubric of '*Vom wahren Wesen der Kinderseele*' ['The True

Nature of the Child Mind'], edited by Frau Dr. H. von Hug-Hellmuth.

20. [*Footnote added* 1919:] An observation made by a parent who had a knowledge of psychoanalysis caught the actual moment at which his highly intelligent four-year-old daughter perceived the distinction between being 'gone' and being 'dead'. The little girl had been troublesome at meal-time and noticed that one of the maids at the pension where they were staying was looking at her askance. 'I wish Josefine was dead,' was the child's comment to her father. 'Why dead?' enquired her father soothingly; 'wouldn't it do if she went away?' 'No,' replied the child; 'then she'd come back again.' The unbounded self-love (the narcissism) of children regards any interference as an act of *lèse majesté*; and their feelings demand (like the Draconian code) that any such crime shall receive the one form of punishment which admits of no degrees.

21. [*Footnote added* 1925:] The situation is often obscured by the emergence of a self-punitive impulse, which threatens the dreamer, by way of a moral reaction, with the loss of the parent whom he loves.

22. [*Footnote added* 1909:] Or so he is reported to have done according to some myths. According to others, emasculation was only carried out by Kronos on his father Uranus.

23. [Freud's views on this point were later modified, Cf. Freud, 1925*j* and 1931*b*.]

24. [The German names for these animals are very much alike: '*Luchs*' and '*Fuchs*'.]

25. [*Footnote added* 1914:] None of the findings of psycho-analytic research has provoked such embittered denials, such fierce opposition – or such amusing contortions – on the part of critics as this indication of the childhood impulses towards incest which persist in the unconscious. An attempt has even

been made recently to make out, in the face of all experience, that the incest should only be taken as 'symbolic'. – Ferenczi (1912) has proposed an ingenious 'over-interpretation' of the Oedipus myth, based on a passage in one of Schopenhauer's letters. – [*Added* 1919:] Later studies have shown that the 'Oedipus complex', which was touched upon for the first time in the above paragraphs in the *Interpretation of Dreams*, throws a light of undreamt-of importance on the history of the human race and the evolution of religion and morality. (See my *Totem and Taboo*, 1912–13 [Essay IV].) – [Actually the gist of this discussion of the Oedipus complex and of the *Oedipus Rex*, as well as of what follows on the subject of *Hamlet*, had already been put forward by Freud in a letter to Fliess as early as October 15th, 1897. (See Freud, 1950*a*, Letter 71.) A still earlier hint at the discovery of the Oedipus complex was included in a letter of May 31st, 1897. (Ibid., Draft N.) – The actual term 'Oedipus complex' seems to have been first used by Freud in his published writings in the first of his 'Contributions to the Psychology of Love' (1910*h*).]

26. [Cf. *Standard Ed.*, 5, 555 f.]

27. [Cf. *Standard Ed.*, 4, 235 ff.]

28. (Cf. my little daughter Anna's dream of strawberries on p. 130 [*Standard Ed.*, 4])

29. [See *Standard Ed.*, 5, 441 ff.]

30. [See *Standard Ed.*, 4, 116]

31. [*Footnote added* 1919:] The above indications of a psycho-analytic explanation of *Hamlet* have since been amplified by Ernest Jones and defended against the alternative views put forward in the literature of the subject. (See Jones, 1910*a* [and, in a completer form, 1949].) – [*Added* 1930:] Incidentally, I have in the meantime ceased to believe that the author of Shakespeare's works was the man from Stratford.

[See Freud, 1930e.] – [Added 1919:] Further attempts at an analysis of *Macbeth* will be found in a paper of mine [Freud, 1916d] and in one by Jekels (1917).

32. [Though in fact it was correct. He was an eighteenth-century follower of Rousseau.]

33. [*Footnote added* 1911:] When Ernest Jones was giving a scientific lecture on the egoism of dreams before an American audience, a learned lady objected to this unscientific generalization, saying that the author of the present work could only judge of the dreams of Austrians and had no business to speak of the dreams of Americans. So far as she was concerned, she was certain that all her dreams were strictly altruistic. – [*Added* 1925:] By way of excuse for this patriotic lady, I may remark that the statement that dreams are entirely egoistic [p. 118] must not be misunderstood. Since anything whatever that occurs in preconscious thought can pass into a dream (whether into its actual content or into the latent dream-thoughts) that possibility is equally open to altruistic impulses. In the same way, an affectionate or erotic impulse towards someone else, if it is present in the unconscious, can appear in a dream.

34. [This dream is further discussed on pp. 555 and 560, *Standard Ed.,* 5]

35. [*Footnote added* 1925:] Analytic research has shown us that in addition to pleasure derived from the organs concerned, there is another factor which contributes to the delight taken by children in acrobatic performances and to their repetition in hysterical attacks. This other factor is a memory-image, often unconscious, of an observation of sexual intercourse, whether between human beings or animals.

36. [Cf. *Standard Ed.,* 4, 37 f.]

37. [Cf. ibid., 237–8]

38. (See ibid., 17)

39. A young medical colleague, who is quite free from any kind of nervous trouble, has given me the following information on this point: 'I know from my own experience that in my childhood I had a peculiar sensation in my genitals when I was on a swing and especially when the downward motion reached its greatest momentum. And though I cannot say I really enjoyed this sensation I must describe it as a pleasurable one.' – Patients have often told me that the first pleasurable erections that they can remember occurred in their boyhood while they were climbing about. – psychoanalysis makes it perfectly certain that the first sexual impulses frequently have their roots in games involving romping and wrestling played during childhood. [This topic was elaborated by Freud in the last section of the second of his *Three Essays on the Theory of Sexuality* (1905*d*).]

© Time life pictures/Mansell

SIGMUND FREUD was born in Freiberg, Moravia in 1856. Having qualified as a medical doctor in Vienna in 1881, Freud specialised in neuropathology which led him to study hysteria and its causes. Freud's clinical work in this area would encourage him to develop his pioneering concept of Psychoanalysis.

Through Psychoanalysis Freud was able to attribute the complexities of human behaviour and development to the various levels, and drives, of the Unconscious. His work was considered highly controversial, and owing to its scandalous conclusions about human nature, many of Freud's theories, including those on the Oedipus Complex, the death drive, the Ego, the Id and the Super-Ego, have entered our collective consciousness. His work was widely appropriated by writers and artists for whom Psychoanalysis offered a liberating perspective on human nature.

Freud eventually left Austria in 1938 to escape the Nazis. He settled in the UK, where he died a year later. While many of his theories have fallen out of practical application, Freud remains one of the pillars of 20th-century science and literature.

RECOMMENDED BOOKS BY SIGMUND FREUD:

The Essentials of Psycho-Analysis
The Standard Edition of the Complete Psychological Works of Sigmund Freud, Volumes IV-V: The Interpretation of Dreams

How do we realise our Dreams?

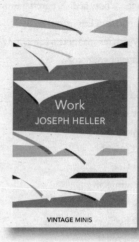

Work
JOSEPH HELLER

VINTAGE MINIS

Money
YUVAL NOAH HARARI

VINTAGE MINIS

Language
XIAOLU GUO

VINTAGE MINIS

Friendship
ROSE TREMAIN

VINTAGE MINIS

VINTAGE MINIS

The Vintage Minis bring you some of the world's greatest writers
on the experiences that make us human. These stylish, entertaining
little books explore the whole spectrum of life – from birth to
death, and everything in between. Which means there's something
here for everyone, whatever your story.

vintageminis.co.uk